She Rises

Overcoming Sexual Abuse & Domestic Violence
What All Women Want To Know

Kayla Hayes & Alisa Divine

Personal Power Press, Inc.
Bay City, Michigan

She Rises

Overcoming Sexual Abuse & Domestic Violence
What All Women Want To Know

© 2020 by Kayla Hayes, Alisa Divine and
Personal Power Press

Library of Congress Control Number: 2020923247

ISBN: 978-0-9821568-0-3

All rights reserved. Printed in the United States of America. No part of this publication may be reproduced, stored in a retrieval system, or transmitted in any form or by any means, electronic, mechanical, photocopying, recording or otherwise, without the written permission of the publisher.

Printed in the United States of America

Personal Power Press, Inc.
Bay City, MI 48706

Cover Photography By:
Alisa Divine

Kayla's lipcolor: LOUD
https://speakcosmetics.com

Disclaimer: The authors and publisher have utilized their best efforts in preparing the information in this book. The stories in this book are experiences and recollections. Some names may have been changed.

Table of Contents

Foreword 1

Introduction 3

Part I: Sexual Abuse & Domestic Violence 7

Chapter 1. Hush Money 8
Chapter 2. The Sexual Abuse 12
Chapter 3. The First Trial 14
Chapter 4. The Second Trial 20
Chapter 5. The Domestic Violence 23
Chapter 6. The Attack 36
Chapter 7. After The Attack 42
Chapter 8. The Healing Process 51
Chapter 9. She Rises & Advocacy 60

Part II: A Guide to Overcoming Abuse 65

How to Use This 66
Chapter 1. Heal What Hurts 68
Chapter 2. Identify What You Want 79
Chapter 3. Master Your Mindset 84
Chapter 4. Build Confidence 89
Chapter 5. Turn Pain into Power 96
Chapter 6. Relationship Red Flags vs Mistakes 103
Chapter 7. Final Words 105

About The Authors 107

Foreword

By Brian N. Boland, MD

Every patient has a story . . . child with leukemia, a gunshot wound to the chest, a car accident resulting in paralysis, and a boyfriend biting his girlfriend's lip off.

I completed a five-year general surgery residency before becoming a plastic surgeon. We don't get emotionally attached to our patients because we can't. Surgeons learn to be empathetic without becoming immersed in their patients' personal stories. It's a way to treat patients objectively and stay focused on the solution. If we revel in the stories, we become emotionally drained, we cannot sleep, we cannot do our jobs, and we fail our patients.

However, there are exceptions to every rule, and in this case, every patient. Kayla's story crushed my heart from the first time we met in the emergency department. She was the girl next door — young, relatable, unassuming. She could have easily been my sister or my friend.

There is a well-known theory that if you take a frog and put it in a pot of boiling water, it will jump out. But if you put a frog in tepid water and gradually heat it up, the frog stays put and ultimately succumbs to the boiling water and dies. I believe this theory is similar to Kayla's experience. The situation she found herself in had become dire without her even knowing it. The pot was boiling...

As Kayla's surgeon, I am honored to be a part of her new story. After multiple surgeries, procedures, and treatments, she is healing the scars that were created on the day we met. As her smile has returned, so has mine. I have watched Kayla transform from a young girl into a spokesperson for domestic violence awareness, letting other women know they are not alone, they don't have to stay in abusive relationships, and they can create new beginnings. She is now a resilient woman with a story, a platform, a book, a following, with more maturity and life experience than most of us will have in our lifetime.

After a tragedy that could have easily kept her down, Kayla moved forward with one foot in front of the other. Now she is running. And this is only the beginning...

Brian N. Boland, MD
Board Certified Plastic Surgeon
Greenville, SC

Introduction
By Alisa Divine

She could have been my daughter.

Kayla is slightly younger than my firstborn.

Her shocking photo and story link came across my Facebook newsfeed. Intuitively, I knew it was domestic violence. I felt compelled to find out what happened to her. I clicked on the link to read and upon doing so, I felt sick. Even though I was familiar with other harrowing stories, I still could not believe what I read.

I was working on an anthology, *#SheWins: Harrowing Stories From Women Who Survived Domestic Abuse*, including stories and photographs of 20 women from around the world. The draft was complete. Until I read that post written by Kayla Hayes about her domestic violence experience. I wanted to do something! I just wanted to scoop her up. I wanted to protect her. I wanted to reach out to her. I wanted to know her.

Part of me resisted, I was so close to going to print with the book. But I could not get Kayla out of my mind. I decided to message her and tell her about the book. She responded with interest. And although I didn't know Kayla's full story, I knew there was something significant about her. We set up an interview over Zoom and she agreed to join in *#SheWins*.

It was more than a year after *#SheWins* was published when Kayla reached out to me — asking if I could help her write a book. She disclosed the sexual abuse she endured as a child. She wanted to let others know how that set her up for more devastation. The trauma, the self-hate, and the lack of confidence she experienced, as a result of the early abuse, led her to choose a boyfriend who was broken and abusive. And it kept her in the relationship after she knew it was harmful to her.

My heart hurt.

Yet I knew. I knew I could help her tell a story of turning pain into power. Of overcoming her obstacles and turning them into opportunities. I knew that by Kayla sharing her story, she could inspire other young women to heal their hurts and to prevent toxic relationships. I held a vision of her speaking in high schools and colleges across the country. I envisioned her changing lives.

At the age of 22 — she is them. Kayla is a person that young women can relate to. According to the National Coalition Against Domestic Violence, women between the ages of 18-24 are most commonly abused by an intimate partner.

And she is me — too. I entered an abusive relationship at the age of 16, and married him at 21. Although I left multiple times, I didn't leave for good until I was 35. The long-lasting effects disturbed the core of my being as a woman. I had to unravel who I was that led me to accept something toxic. I went through my own journey of healing and overcoming.

I learned to define my boundaries, build my confidence, love myself, and build something bigger than my pain — from scratch.

And I did it in the exact way I wanted — with peace and freedom — what I believe all survivors of abuse yearn for.

Through my journey, I became the founder of The More Than Beautiful Project™, where I passionately coach women to embody more than their beauty. I believe women also want a strong mindset, an abundance of confidence, a positive self-image, healthy relationships, the know-how to overcome obstacles and to live satisfying lives.

My path continued and I became CEO of Personal Power Press, where I provide a platform for others to write and publish their stories. I've authored multiple books. And I coach women to turn their pain into power and position themselves as leaders in the world.

My wish for you, after experiencing this book is that you:

- Heal your hurts — so you can feel freedom and peace.
- Identify what you want in life. Love again. Trust again. And believe in the best.
- Master your mindset. It can be the foundation for growth.
- Build confidence and become so strong in who you are. Know you are worthy of the best.
- Turn your pain into power. And once you do that, keep going and help someone else. Live a life filled with meaning and purpose.
- Only accept healthy relationships from this point on.

Kayla could be my daughter. She could be your daughter. She could be your sister.

She could be you.

Sexual assault and domestic violence are everyone's issues. If it hasn't happened to you — it's happened to someone you know.

What if we all take responsibility to heal what hurts within and then move beyond to ultimately create something bigger?

The awareness and tools to do this — are in your hands, right now.

Will you join us?

Part I:

Sexual Abuse & Domestic Violence

Chapter 1

Hush Money

The summer days of my childhood were often spent with my paternal grandparents.

It was fun during the day.

It was awful at night.

One lazy afternoon at my grandparents' house, I walked down the trail past the river to my grandfather's shed. I noticed a repulsive smell when walking in. I asked what it was and he told me he was making apple cider. I saw that he had an elaborate system set up.

But what *I remember* — was grandfather often talking about Moonshine. And he talked about how strong it was. I actually never saw him drink apple cider.

He didn't fit the profile of an apple cider-making Grandpa.

He was a Moonshine Grandpa.

Moonshine disgusts me.

I was raised by a single mom. I didn't have much family around except for my father's mom and her husband. They helped my mom out a lot. I was there almost every weekend and they would also pick me up from school until my mom was done with work. Visiting my grandparents were the only times I saw my half-brother and sister. I didn't have contact with my dad and going to my grandparents' house meant also spending quality time with my siblings.

My grandmother took me to Ohio, from South Carolina to see her mom and sister, nieces and nephews. We spent a lot of time traveling and enjoying family time together.

They showered me with gifts. It felt like "The Dream Life" when I was with them. They took me on a cruise at 10 years old. I thought they were showing me how much they loved me. The gifts poured in all the time.

Everyone thought I was my grandparents' favorite because they always had me over there. There were plenty of things to do. There was a river nearby for us to go tubing. They had a pool. They bought us go-karts and we enjoyed riding through the woods. My grandmother and I played hide and seek through the woods and around the house. We always went out to eat. I got to mow the lawn. I got to ride on tractors. I got to do a lot of "big kid" stuff.

They scuba dived often and even took me to get scuba certified. We did that in Lake Jocassee. It was so much fun. I got to explore the bottom of the lake. They kept me busy. And I had my own room at their house.

Now, I think of it all as — hush money.

In the evenings, we kids would go out to the pool. Once, we saw the flame of a cigarette being lit from the side porch. Then every time grandfather took a puff of it, we saw the reflection from his glasses. He was staring at us. He had a way of making me feel uncomfortable in my own skin. He gave us girls compliments when we were in our bathing suits. He told me I was his favorite.

There were other odd things that happened. My grandfather used to buy my grandmother these magazines. You could order skimpy bikinis from them. He would try to get me to order bikinis to match hers. At first I thought it was weird because they were extremely skimpy — and I was young. And then I felt confused because I thought it would be fun to match with my grandmother. Like I wanted to trust that I was being taken care of.

It was never about being sexy to me — I was a child — I didn't understand sexy.

My grandmother often talked about her first two marriages. They were both abusive. She was beaten. She drilled that in our heads. That was what we grew up knowing — how badly she was treated. He threw her against the wall, stomped on her chest, then on my dad's chest.

Then she'd go on to say how my step-grandfather, her third husband, lets her buy whatever she wants. She thought he was the man of her dreams. He'd let her do anything she wanted. And he'd give her the money to go do it. All of this added to my confusion.

Chapter 2

The Sexual Abuse

I was a six-year-old when he first touched me. It went on until I was 10.

It felt wrong.

I didn't have the words.

I didn't have the power.

I had no self-esteem.

He took all of it from me.

I woke up from a dead sleep to him whispering in my ear. I couldn't make out half of what he said. I did understand him telling me to spread my legs. And I ignored him. He kept repeating himself. I still ignored him. Then he grabbed both my legs and pulled them apart. He pulled my pants down and began touching me in places I didn't approve of.

I was mortified. And I had no clue what to do.

Then the fingering began. I didn't know what was happening and I was trembling and afraid. He kept pulling me closer to him. It felt wrong. It felt confusing. He reeked of cigarettes. I felt sick. I wanted to run away but I froze. My body was paralyzed.

I don't know why I remember the Dr. Pepper pajama pants he wore — maybe because I associate them with feeling so disgusted and disappointed with him. As he pulled them down, he forced me to touch him.

All while my grandmother was in the same bed!

So many bad thoughts went through my head. I didn't know what was going on. I didn't know why he was doing that. I didn't know if it was normal for grandfathers to do that. I told myself not to cry, that it would be over soon.

I was innocent. I thought it would be the only time. But it wasn't. I always tried to get away from him. And he overpowered me. Once I tried to scream and he let me go. I went outside to where my grandmother and the other kids were.

My emotions were stifled inside me. They were toxic and damaging me. I would spaz out and isolate myself. I felt so very angry and disgusted with myself. Like I was to blame. It was so difficult. I wanted to believe my grandfather truly loved me.

I never wanted to tell. And I wasn't the only one. He also abused my sister and we made a pact not to tell. We promised never to tell our family members — no one. We would keep it between us. We didn't want to hurt our grandmother. We thought we were the problems. We thought it was our fault. We asked each other, "Who are we to ruin the perfect life grandmother thought she had?"

The amount of guilt I felt was overwhelming. I was the oldest and I made my little sister promise never to tell anyone. And then I felt anger towards myself for making that promise.

We made my grandmother's well-being more important than our well-being.

Chapter 3
The First Trial

Kayla and Her Mom

I didn't know how to cope. Deep down the secret I held was poisoning me. I stopped hanging out with my friends. I lost interest in everything I once loved. I used to dance and compete. And I just stopped one day. I told my mom I wanted to quit because I hated wearing tights but it was really because I felt inferior to everyone else. I saw my dance friends bring their families to the competitions. It looked like everyone had the perfect family — except me. I envied them for sure. I refused to go to my grandparents' house. I didn't want to see him. Or hug him. Or be anywhere near him.

I felt different from everyone else my age. And I was. I felt completely alone. It was rough — trying to understand what happened to me. I confessed to my best friend, "I feel like my whole life is a lie." That was all I said. I didn't elaborate on it. I couldn't articulate the lie I held within me for so long. My friend told my mom.

A volcano was bubbling inside me. The pressure built up and ruptured during a fight with my mom. It was after a soccer tournament, when I was 12. We went out to dinner with the team and I wanted nothing to do with any of it. My mom added up my isolation and the comment to my friend, and she questioned me.

Without warning, it erupted from me: "Do you want to know what's wrong with me? IT'S MY GRANDFATHER!"

I ran into the house to my room. I called my sister and let her know that it was finally out. We didn't have to hide it any longer — even though we made the pact not to tell anyone so we wouldn't hurt our grandmother.

My mom called the police that night and since it was a Friday, they told us to come in on Monday morning and file a police report. There were a lot of tears over the weekend.

When my mom and I arrived at the station on Monday, we met with Officer Gary. He took me into a room to discuss what happened and then gave me time alone to write a statement. It was hard to be in a room with a man, even a police officer. I felt fearful of men. I had no positive examples of men in my life. The officer assured my mom and me that my grandfather would be held accountable. He said he would be in contact with us shortly.

Weeks passed and we heard nothing from the police department. My mom called the officer we met with. Nothing. Then she began calling daily. She was sent to voicemail over and over again. Weeks, months, and eventually years passed without any answers. My mom begged and pleaded with the woman who answered the phone to have someone, anyone give us a call back — to give us some possibility that I would get justice.

After two years of getting nowhere through the police department, my mom reached out to a counselor she found online. She knew I needed help. I struggled with my emotions and it affected all areas of my life. She set up a phone call with the counselor and let her know what was happening with me. She informed my mom that she needed to follow up with a call to the Department of Social Services. By doing so, this prompted the police department to investigate further.

Finally, we received a call that my file was being transferred to another officer and we would have an interview at the Julie Valentine Center. My mom and I did not know what to expect. I met with two officers to give my statement again as they recorded it. That was almost three years after filing my initial police report. We were told that they were going to get a warrant signed for my grandfather's arrest. Within hours, we received a phone call that he was taken into custody.

Days later, we got another call at 10:30 a.m. that there was going to be a bail hearing at 2:30 p.m. the same day and it was recommended that we be there. It was also my final soccer tournament of freshman year, a couple of hours away. My mom was very upset that after waiting for years for my voice to be heard — I couldn't be there. I already lost so much of my childhood. Grandfather was arrested in June, 2014.

The wait ensued with weekly follow-up calls by my mom, with no answers on what to expect next. We only knew the case was turned over to the solicitor's office. Nothing happened. In October 2017, we got the call that finally, grandfather was going to trial after being out on bond since 2014. They agreed and set the trial date for May, 2018.

In the months that followed, we were appointed two of the most amazing women to help us through my case. Jackie, the prosecutor, and Rhonda, a victim's advocate. My mom and I worked with them for months to get caught up to speed. Jackie spent countless days gathering all the information and texting us late into the night to ensure she could fight my case to the best of her ability. Rhonda comforted us through the steps and the process. She made up for all the delays in the past. We asked questions and my momma begged for answers on why we were let down. Why it took so long to bring my case to trial. She wanted to know how to prevent this same thing from happening to anyone else.

We learned that the officer we originally filed the report with left the department abruptly with my file on his desk, among other things. My file was eventually found and given to another officer along with 60 plus other cases. The arrest took place once the file moved to the solicitor office, who also left the department. Balls had dropped everywhere from 2012 to 2018. It wasn't until a new solicitor came into the department that the mess was cleared.

My sister also came forward in January, 2018 and additional charges were brought against our grandfather. Grandfather's attorney fought for the cases to be tried separately and he won. My case was first, the trial date arrived.

I had to stand up and tell everyone, random strangers, what he did to me as a child.

During the trial, the defense spent all their time and energy making it a "baby daddy" problem. They used Facebook messages prior to 2012 where my mom was messaging a cousin saying that my confidence was really low because I had not seen my father in a number of days. They used that against us. They accused my mom of going after money from my father. They put my father on the stand and made it about him. It was not about my father! It was a trial for my grandfather sexually abusing me! My six-year silence was even used as an excuse against me. Rhonda fought like a bulldog. She was great at countering those pieces. She was incredible.

There were holes, however. The officer that was on the stand could not answer the questions he was being asked. It was his job to know that information and he failed to be prepared. He stated he never had training in childhood sexual abuse and he had been given an abundance of cases.

In the end, the jury found grandfather "not guilty." My mom and I were devastated. Years of fighting, standing up for what's right, years spent making sure that it wouldn't happen to anyone else. Not my baby sister, not my cousin, not anyone. It seemed wasted. Hearing "not guilty" on all charges felt like a punch to the gut. Did they think I was lying? Why would I make it up? Why did the defense think I was using it to get back at my father?

The police department let us down. Because of them, grandfather walked out from four years of being on bond and a four-day trial — as a free man. And I was the one who felt I was left behind bars, not being validated or really seen for what I experienced.

My mom and I went home after the trial and she received a Facebook message from a stranger. A stranger who also was a jury alternate. This is what it said:

I don't know if I should send this, but my feelings were too strong not to. I just want your daughter to know that the three jury alternates felt very strongly and very differently than what was decided. All three of us waited in the courtroom until 7:20 p.m. last night. We are broken-hearted over the verdict, and I will be praying for your family.

All three of us said we would never say "not guilty" no matter what. I think none of the others were as strong a personality as the one that wanted him found not guilty. There was one person that felt strongly not to convict, and everyone else got tired of arguing. That's how I heard it anyway. Very sad.

The defense attorney talked to us last night. He said the fact that they said grandma was right there was one thing that convinced the strong juror it wasn't true. I looked at him and said, 'Well it happened to me with my mom in the same bed asleep.'

I wanted to contact you because I didn't want the girls to think nobody believes them. It should have been a different outcome. I was glad I was there. I was supposed to be…for some reason. It was crazy because what happened to your daughter is almost exactly what happened to me. Mine was my stepdad and mom. Same age and same kind of experiences. I didn't prosecute him because my mom wanted to stay with him, and I wanted her to be happy. But I can tell you, I was so disappointed with the outcome.

We felt some peace after receiving that message.

Chapter 4

The Second Trial

My case was over, but my sister's case still needed to go to trial. The prosecutor and the advocate promised to fight just as hard as in my case. We questioned how there could be a different outcome. My mom spent years fighting for me, taking me to counseling, fighting for my voice to be heard. My sister had a statement. She didn't have all the other pieces that I had. But she would have one piece that I didn't. The prosecutor ensured that the second trial would have the transcripts from my trial as evidence.

At the midpoint of the second trial, my grandfather's story began to unravel. He lied so much he couldn't keep the lies straight. After day three, prior to the jury deliberations, he pled guilty to the lesser charge of assault and battery, first degree. I attended the trial each day. He never admitted fully to what he did to my sister and me. Even so, finally, it felt like he was being held accountable.

Hearing him admit he was guilty of something — spoke volumes to me that he was guilty of all of the charges.

I didn't get the closure that I wanted from my case. It was up to 12 jurors to decide whether or not I got the justice I desperately searched for. And yet in the end, hearing him admit that he was guilty — was more satisfying to me than 12 random strangers validating my abuse. He was sentenced to 10 years which was suspended to five years with only having to serve 50 percent.

Through it all, my grandmother stood beside my grandfather. She failed my sister and me. She didn't keep us safe. She didn't protect us. She sent us the message that a man was more important to her than us. She will have to live with her choices.

I have never liked drama and I didn't want to cause a wedge between families — ultimately though that's what happened. I didn't want to tell and hurt my grandmother. And to make the situation more difficult, my grandfather's father was elderly and recently lost his wife. He was heartbroken, losing her. I looked up to him a lot. He always made time for me. We traveled together too. I didn't want to hurt him. I definitely didn't want to hurt my grandmother. And who was I to bring more sadness to my family when they were already going through difficult times?

I also knew there would be consequences for me. When I finally came out, I literally felt that I lost everything. My grandmother completely disowned me. I went from seeing her on a daily basis, to not hearing a word from her. In fact, she told my family that I quit talking to her. But looking back now, I know I didn't lose anything. That was not the family I needed. My grandmother took his side. She made him more important than us. I couldn't believe my grandmother even got up on the stand and lied for him. If she could betray my trust and do horrid things to defend her husband's actions — then I lost someone who was no good for me in anyway.

The thing was, I believe she knew the whole time. She was in the room, right there, one of the times when it happened. She was always in the house or outside somewhere during the other times. It felt so weird.

Grandfather was the type of man to make sexual, nasty jokes to my mom when she was a teenager — until the last time we were with him. My mom always figured he only directed that towards her, she was 18 when she had me. She didn't think he would ever do anything to me.

She trusted him.

As kids, we played hide and seek with my grandparents. We'd find DVDs upon DVDs of pornographic videos under his bed. And they were on his computer too. He was a sick human being when it came to sex. He was gross. He molested little kids.

Through my tween and teen years, I was afraid of all older men. When they looked at me, I felt I had to cower down to them. I felt ashamed of myself and ashamed of my family. I felt everything was my fault. I deserved it — whatever it was — for whatever I ever did. I was young, maybe I asked for it in some way? As a trusted adult, he could convince me anything was my fault and I believed him. He could convince me to not tell through his commentary and I kept it hushed. It felt dirty. It felt like dragging a heavy weight around with me. My life didn't feel authentic, it felt fake. It felt like my life was a lie. I worried as a teen that no boy would ever want me. I was "used goods." Who would want to love me after I went through *that*?

There are times now when I don't want to be touched at all. It still affects me. Sometimes I don't even want someone to touch my arm — something which seems so simple.

The older I got, the angrier I got. I didn't want to live to be 80 years old, feeling that way.

I wanted to believe that my grandparents just wanted to spoil me — instead of what really happened — they threw gifts at me to keep me quiet over what took place behind their doors. It was sickening.

To this day — it still blows my mind — all I lost because of him. Because of his actions.

Chapter 5
The Domestic Violence

Aaron was different from my high school friends. They had big homes, material things and toys, and families with a mom and dad. I didn't have any of those. He didn't care.

What I did have was a mother who gave me everything I needed and wanted— and if she couldn't, she worked her ass off until she could. One of her greatest accomplishments was purchasing a house when I was in the third grade.

It was an old mill house. I was beyond proud of her. She left her parents' house at 16 years old with nothing but the clothes on her back. After much hard work, she was able to buy the house. It was the perfect starter home for mom and me. It was the fear of judgment though, that kept me from bringing friends over. I already held so much worry and anxiety over what others thought. The first time I did have a friend over, he told everyone afterwards that I lived in a "trap house." But it wasn't. I was proud of my mom for what she did for us and yet I was judged. It felt hard. It seemed like that was a defining moment for me and also a reason why I didn't want to date through high school. I still was worried about my past and I wasn't secure in who I was. I worried that someone would find out about my past. I worried what they would say and if they would judge me. I'm sure it showed.

When I met Aaron the summer before my senior year, it just felt so easy to be with him. I didn't feel as insecure. I didn't worry about my past as much.

I saw Aaron at a party but we didn't talk to each other. I was 17 and he was 21. A week later a friend called me and said Aaron was at a mutual friend's house and he wanted me to come over. I went over to hang out and we started talking. He was kind and a gentleman. It seemed like older guys were pushy but he wasn't like that. We started hanging out as a couple.

Soon after we coupled up, he planned to go out of town for the weekend to visit his grandparents and cousins. The Thursday before he began acting strangely. He was out with friends, drinking, and I told him to have a good night and be careful. I didn't hear back from him. I sent him a few texts over the weekend but got no response until Monday evening. That was when he told me he started talking to his ex-girlfriend, while at the beach over the weekend. He told me to leave him alone. And I did.

A week later, he called me. He was freaking out. He went to a Greenville Drive baseball game with his ex-girlfriend, now girlfriend. And they got into a fight. He was arrested for public intoxication. He gave me one story. She told me another story. I believed the girlfriend's side because I think what Aaron told me was twisted so he looked like the victim and I would feel sorry for him. There were beer cans thrown between them and necklaces ripped off.

I was naive. And he was "playing gentle," like he did the first time I met him. I agreed to see him once he got out of jail. He was there less than 24 hours, but he swore up and down he was never going back. He said it was the worst place he had ever been.

Yet when he got out, he messaged people he met while in jail. "Hey man, it's me. I was in the county jail with you, how've you been? Let's hang out," he texted. He thought it was funny. He quickly forgot it was the worst place.

We ended up back together.

But he didn't take responsibility in relationships. It seemed that all of his exes were crazy and the cause for his issues. He once told me when we were dating to never hit him in the face. I asked him if someone did that to him before. He said yes, a girl slapped him in the face. But I later discovered, he actually punched her in the jaw and dislocated it. The tables were always turned. Stories were always twisted. He thought he was a "real man" because he admitted his wrongs and pushed past them. Admitting it was one step. Changing his actions was another step.

He talked big but he didn't do the real work. The inside work.

Aaron would joke with me. Only they weren't jokes — his comments were demeaning. If I didn't want him to touch me — or hug me — he couldn't handle it. He brought up the sexual abuse I endured as a child. "Oh you don't want me to touch you because you miss those old-man fingers touching you. You were 'fondled.'"

His words stuck with me.

They added to my pain. They dominated my actions. I felt that because Aaron was older than me, I had to cower down to him and give him what he wanted. That's what I had to do when I was young. I didn't have a fighting chance then — so why would I have a fighting chance with Aaron? He always sought dominance. To be "large and in charge."

The threat of physical abuse came early in our relationship. One night at his grandma's retirement party, we got into an argument. I was "being quiet" and he didn't like it. He called me a "bitch" and made such an issue out of it that we left. He accused me of ruining the whole night. We walked down a big hill. I had a dress and high heels on. He was yelling at me, then all of the sudden he stopped. I turned around as he fell to the ground, in an attempt to drop-kick me. But my timing was perfect and I moved before he could. After that I couldn't help but wonder if it was his intention for me to face plant the ground and tumble down the hill. Just because he was angry.

He also cheated on me the night before his best friend's wedding. He got very drunk with the guys and blew up my phone until 2 a.m. calling me a whore and accusing me of cheating because I wasn't answering. I was home, asleep. He was the one who cheated with the bridesmaid he walked down the aisle with the next day.

At the wedding, everyone I sat with knew what happened but no one said a word to me. I had a terrible gut feeling and tried to push it aside believing nothing was wrong. But after the wedding when he took me to his hotel room to get his things, there were feminine items everywhere. He said they belonged to the bridesmaids who used his room to get ready for the ceremony. So I trusted him.

To my own harm, I never trusted my own gut feelings.

Aaron only admitted what happened when he knew he might get caught. I was going to get my hair done Monday afternoon by one of the girls he and his friends knew. He freaked out around lunch time and texted me while I was at school. He confessed he messed up and cheated on me. I bet he thought the girl who was cutting my hair would tell me. She had no idea and was blown away when I told her. I think he always had a guilty conscience.

Aaron also was materialistic. He had a new truck and traded it in for a newer 2016 Four Runner. It didn't matter if he needed five co-signers to get it; he bullied the co-signers until they agreed to sign. He wanted everything to be brand new and top of the line. He always tried to outdo everything and everyone. When he was interested in something, he went in hard. He bought a $2,000 bicycle and then added extras to it even though he couldn't afford to buy it himself. It was like an obsession that his possessions made him more important.

He craved attention. Once I went to the doctor with him and he was prescribed Zoloft. He went around bragging about it. He told people the doctor thought he was going to "off" himself so he gave him a drug. He went on to say he felt great and was doing so well. He got the attention he was looking for.

He may have looked like a stand-up guy, a Christian with cross tattoos — but he was hypocritical. He criticized me, saying I was doing wrong by the Bible. "This is what the Bible says," and "This is how you're supposed to do it." He made me feel worse about myself.

Even every holiday spent with him was all about him. It didn't matter what holiday. Aaron was extremely greedy. He wasn't grateful. He wanted Costa sunglasses and with the help of my mom, I bought them for him. They didn't have the maximum polarization that he wanted so he left them at my house and then bitched — telling me to send them back and get him the right ones. They were at my house for three months and I never heard a thank you. Another time he took me to the mall and told me to pick out any purse that I wanted — it didn't matter how much it cost. I found out later, he asked my mom for money to pay for it because he couldn't afford to buy me a Christmas present.

Then our relationship turned physical. After our New Year's party, he body slammed the door I was standing behind. It knocked me over into a wooden bed frame. I had a gash on my nose and a black eye. I made up a story that I ran into a door when a friend was opening it. I didn't want him to get into trouble. He made absurd jokes when I felt upset about how badly I looked. He said, "Well you're the dumb ass that let that girl hit you with the door."

After this happened I went to school and it was like I was the joke of the week. Clearly hurting, I had the busted face and instead of someone just genuinely asking me, "Are you ok?" "Can I help in some way?" — I received laughter. Maybe I would've spoken up about the truth then. Maybe and maybe not, but that could have been such an essential thing to know that I wasn't alone. That someone cared. Instead, people behind me in class started group chats saying, "Well, if she wants to let her boyfriend beat on her then that's her own issue." I just remember going in the bathroom stall and bawling my eyes out.

I feel that experience changed who I am today. I always try my best to notice things in people and ask them something as simple as, "Are you ok?" That way I feel as though I do what I can to let them know that someone is there for them. I want to be the friend that I wish I would have had.

The first time I tried breaking it off with him, I had the purse he bought me in the car. Aaron and I planned to go out to eat with a friend for her birthday when we got into an argument, I don't remember over what. I told him to just leave — to drop me off and I'd find my own way home. But instead he came into the restaurant. I made excuses for him and told my friend he was having a bad day. Then he started drinking and caused a scene, bringing all the attention back to him. We left. I got into my car and we argued even more. He followed me to a gas station. I told him I was done, that I couldn't do it anymore. He asked me for the purse. I told him he could have it back after I took all my stuff out of it.

Next thing I knew, Aaron jerked me out of my car by my hair. And he slammed me up against my back door. He grabbed the purse, dumped it out and took my phone. He refused to give it back. That was another black eye. It took a long time to talk him out of it. Finally I got my phone and my stuff back. I told him we could figure it out. Every time I tried to leave the relationship — something happened to me and I was fearful.

My mom and I were criticized — that we should have seen the warning signs. That I should have gotten out of the relationship earlier. But when I did see the signs, I tried to get out. And I couldn't see how I could actually get away from him. He was persistent. He didn't take "no" for an answer. I felt there was no possibility of it.

Every time he harassed me or hurt me, he brought me cards, letters and even a book about girls working through their anxiety and depression. At times, it felt meaningful. But when I read them now — I realize it was all the same. He was always sorry he hurt me. And he always promised to be "slow-to-anger" the next time.

Aaron definitely had a way with words.

He was convincing. And yet there was always a next time.

During our relationship, he pushed me to a breaking point. It was either choose him or listen to my mom who did not want me to talk to him. She even took my phone away. I lost part of myself when I was with him. And then I lost myself completely. If I would have stayed with him longer, I would have only had him. He wasn't going to share me with anyone. He was constantly blowing up my phone asking me where I was going and who was I with. He had a tracking app on my phone, and if I was in an area he wasn't familiar with, it set him off.

Finally, I had enough of it all. I filled out papers for a restraining order because he wouldn't stop harassing me. I was told it could take up to two months to make it permanent and I would have to face him in court. I didn't want to face him and I didn't want to wait two months, so I dropped the restraining order. In the meantime, I got a no trespassing order for our home and my workplace. We also put up cameras so we could have proof that he came back in violation of the order. I still have the video of him banging on the front door, looking through windows, giving up, driving off and then seeing me and coming back to beat on the door again. He harassed me at work as well.

He was not home when he was served with the no trespassing order so his grandmother signed for him. Then he sent my mom a text message saying, "I got your cute little message today." He also added a kissy-face emoji to the text. Of course, he came back to my house and beat on my door but by the time Police Officer Pennant got there, Aaron had left. When the officer telephoned him in front of me and asked him if he knew about the order, he lied, saying he knew nothing about it. The officer told him to "move on" and leave me alone before more issues arose.

A couple of days later, he showed up again at my house. I blocked his number. But he found ways around it and texted me from his friends' phones by downloading different apps.

He would not leave me alone.

It was always something. When he wanted the phone back that he supposedly bought me, I told him I would leave it somewhere and he could come pick it up after I left. He called me when he was driving through my neighborhood. He said if he ever found me, he would kill me.

When I heard those words come from his mouth — I should have realized the seriousness, the lethality.

This was not a game.

It was real life.

My life.

He tried to win me back. Playing the pity party attendee, he talked about wanting to kill himself. He couldn't live to see another day because his heart was empty. So when he was house sitting for his cousins and asked me to join him – of course I took his words seriously and I did.

He was sloppy drunk. He could hardly stand. He had flowers and my favorite chocolates.

But I was done. I drew the line.

After the breakup, he posted my business on Instagram to get a reaction:

Don't trust a girl who's been through some stupid crap being molested and with daddy issues. Because they will talk to someone behind your back and make up some stupid crap about how they need to find themselves. Even when you messed up during an argument they'll run away to that other person. Yeah y'all know who this is about and I'm done for my rant but Kayla Hayes doesn't mean crap to me anymore.

And:

Let me tell everyone about someone I know. She went behind my back to meet some new guy and told me she needed time for herself and blah blah. She tries to make everyone feel sorry for her because of what her grandpa did to her and the fact that her dad left her and she's really good at this so be warned because I fell for it and I'm no saint, trust me. It was my fault but to go behind someone's back that's trying to fix things and tries so hard is like a knife in the back. Kayla Hayes doesn't mean crap to me anymore. No matter how hard you try she's gonna run away so be warned everyone. Because she'll use her past and crap to make you feel sorry for her and that is the end of my rant, goodnight.

I was completely embarrassed and mortified that he posted about what happened with my grandfather. I was able to delete the first post and then he posted it again. Then he started sending me pictures of the likes and comments and telling me: "Everyone in Simpsonville screenshot it and your world is about to crash. No one likes you. My phone has been blowing up. It might not be today or tomorrow or next year but one day I'll see you. You're a rat, have an awesome night. Love ya baby girl lol." Then he added that he did not initiate the meet up.

Weeks passed. Preparations were underway for the case against my grandfather and I was consumed with the details. It was emotional every day. It was scary. It was heart-breaking. Luckily, my dog Ella was like my saving grace. I didn't realize it at the time but she helped me take my focus off of the trial and the relationship, and put it on something else. She became my little best friend. I took her everywhere with me. I could say that I gained the courage to leave the relationship with Aaron just shortly after I got her. She was a big distraction and a channel for me to give my love to someone else.

In the meantime, I wanted the break with Aaron to be complete but I still had a few of his good things. I wanted to leave them somewhere for him to pick up — I had no intention to meet him or get back together. Just simply drop his stuff off so he could have it back. It was going to be a step of closure for me, in a way, getting rid of his stuff. But I wanted to do it without seeing him. I texted him on a Friday night and asked him if he wanted any of his things back. He texted back and said he was joining the Navy. He continued saying he really wanted to see me before he left.

Repeatedly.

I refused and kept saying I wished him the best. I was glad that he had his head on straight and he was doing better. But he said I was trying to get back together with him. He said I confused him. But it wasn't like that — I only wished him well. After a while I decided to give him a chance to "right his wrongs" or fix the damage and leave it as good as possible in case something happened to him in the Navy. The only reason I even ended up agreeing was so we didn't end on bad terms.

We met in the parking lot that night. He was playing with my mind. He thought that I was going to give in like I used to. Later that night he blew up my phone. I asked him, "Are we going to start this again?" His response, "still protective as shit." Then he told me to call him because there was a lot wrong. I asked how all of the sudden, he had a lot going wrong. Then he tried to make me feel guilty saying, "I'd make time if it were you."

I texted the next morning and told him that we needed to get this done. Aka — say goodbye and move on. We met up. Again, he thought I was trying to get back together with him. He tried to convince me to go out of town with him for Saturday night and even take my dog. She was a puppy at the time and could fit in a pocketbook. He insisted. He felt there was still something between us. He said if there was, he didn't want to let it go. He knew Charleston was my happy place. It was a place we enjoyed going to together. My mom was out of town and he wanted to go before she got back on Sunday.

After our meeting early that morning, he began sending me quotes:

I'd rather have bad times with you than good times with someone else.

I'd rather be beside you in a storm than safe and warm by myself.

I'd rather have bad times together than to have it easy apart.

I'd rather have the one who warms my heart.

Our sparkle could never go out.

He kept sending me those kinds of things.

Although he said he was going into the Navy, he sent me a picture of an application he never finished and asked me how to do a specific math problem. It never dawned on me that he hadn't actually turned the application in and he wasn't leaving in two weeks, like he said.

He told me that he felt like we still should go to Charleston, even if it would be the last time we talked or did anything together. He said, "One final getaway could be the best thing for us, or it could show us something." He sent me a few more texts and asked if I wanted breakfast or Starbucks. I told him no, I was sick to my stomach. "Well, I was really looking forward to seeing you. Anyway, I could come by? Maybe cut off the camera?" he asked. I went back to sleep.

I woke up to three separate texts.

"Meet me at the mill."

"In 30 mins."

"I really don't wanna show up to your house."

A few minutes later, I said ok. Then I tried to change the subject and talked about my dog.

He ignored it. He said he was coming over and asked where the cameras were.

I said no. I would be dead if he showed up and my mom saw him here. So we met down the street from my house in a parking lot.

He acted nervous because he kept asking me to bring him a bottle of water. Then he told me, "Just c'mon!"

Chapter 6

The Attack

October 21, 2017, the day of the attack is still very vivid to me. Almost like I relive it daily. When I close my eyes, I can see it happening again and again and again.

Somehow — my intuition — told me not to park next to him, in case I needed to get away. It was odd, since I never had that thought before. He pulled in the driveway in front of me. He was already parked and I parked several spots away. I was thrown off and didn't know what to do. I got into his car.

He had flowers and two cards. One of the cards said something about getting back together again when I was ready. The front of the card talked about kisses lasting forever. It was a card he had also given me before. I said the card was cute and I didn't say anything else. That was it.

About five minutes later, he asked, "You've got nothing else to say?"

"No, I've already told you we are not getting back together. We've been over for a month and a half," I said.

With full-on rage in his voice, like I'd never heard before, he demanded I "get the fuck out of the car."

And I did. He threw the flowers and the cards at the back of my head as I got out. Then he got out and ran around to the other side of his car to get them. I had made it into my car by then.

I was in a panic and was shaking. I couldn't move. I remember looking down at my leg which was shaking uncontrollably. And when I looked back up he was picking up the flowers and the cards.

Just then my mom texted me. A guy I knew had just been killed. He was helping someone push their car because it broke down and he was hit by another car in the process. My last text to my mom was, "Wcw — it is crazy how fast things happen."

By then Aaron had opened my driver's side door. He leaned in and set the flowers and cards on the seat.

He leaned close, near my cheek, trying to kiss me.

I jerked back and said, "No!"

Maybe that triggered him. He never wanted me to say "no" to him.

I thought he was coming back to force a kiss on me.

But instead I felt him latch on to my lip. He bit down and I felt him tearing it from my face.

My lip and a large chunk of my chin as well.

It was savage.

It happened so quickly.

Faster than I could react, he grabbed me by my shirt and my hair. He dragged me out of my car, ripping one side of my shirt apart.

I screamed with everything I had in me. I was on the ground in between the door and the door frame. Just then Aaron saw there was a man nearby, looking at us. So he slammed the door in my face. Spit the piece of my lip and chin out onto my lap. Then ran to his car and took off.

Somehow — my phone was in my hand. I think the elderly woman who came to my side handed it to me.

Some people think I took selfies. I didn't. The camera was clicking. I was trying to figure out where the piece of flesh came from that was resting on my leg. Even though I felt my lip and chin tear, I couldn't believe they were actually separated from my face.

I remember looking at the camera on my phone and all I could see was blood. My whole face felt numb and there was the burning sensation of fire where he bit me.

There was not much I remember thinking, other than suicide. I was fading in and out. One second I knew what was going on and another I only saw red. Everything was red. All I could think of in the moment was that I would never be able to face the world again. Suicide was my only option. I didn't think I could be fixed. I was already insecure. I couldn't imagine going on. I heard a voice in the back of my head telling me to just kill myself.

The man who called 911 will forever be considered my guardian angel. It was about 12:15 p.m. on a Saturday afternoon and he happened to be taking out the trash. I remember looking up at him.

That man will have to live with the mental and emotional shrapnel of me sitting in a puddle of my blood, 85 percent of my lip and chin on top of my lap. I was covered in asphalt, my clothes as much as torn off me. And I was still trying to understand what had happened. I remember the look of terror on his face.

Both of our lives changed forever.

Guardian Angel Who Called 911

What I want others to know is that domestic violence and teen dating violence — they don't just affect the two people in the relationship. They affect all others who cross each of those two people's paths as well.

Imagine being him.

There also was a sweet, elderly woman who walked out of her nearby home minutes after my attack. She walked onto the scene and did her best to try to comfort me through the blur of activity. She turned my car off while the man was talking with 911 to report what happened.

Police Officers at the Scene of the Attack

I remember Officer Randall coming around the back of the vehicle with Officer Pennant following. Officer Pennant was the same policeman whom I met when Aaron violated the no trespassing order. Officer Randall pulled his walkie talkie out to speak into it. He called in, saying it was more serious than what they were expecting, my lip being completely severed off. He told the EMS to come quickly. Then they gave me a piece of gauze and tried to help me to stay calm. He wanted to find out more details.

Once I got in the ambulance, they asked me to call my mother. I could not bring myself to do it. She was seven hours away, on her first vacation she had ever taken without me. I didn't want to ruin it. Finally, I was on the phone with my mom's friend and I was trying to explain that Aaron bit me, but I couldn't pronounce the words correctly. I became a wreck of emotions again and handed the phone to the lady behind me so she could explain.

I stared out the back window of the ambulance, not sure if we would make it to the hospital. And wishing I didn't, wishing those moments would be my last.

To this day, when I hear or see an ambulance, I feel panic. And I'm brought back to that very day again.

Right after the attack, Aaron was gone. He showed up at my house later with his mom and that's when he was arrested. His mom was confused because Aaron told her that we "nibbled" and he "nibbled" just a little too hard and that's why he had blood all over him. He called me while I was in the ambulance. It was probably when he was on the way back to my house. He called two or three times. I just remember looking at my phone and screaming, "He's calling me? Why is he calling me?" Like he's done enough already! Why is he calling? And he continued to call me when I got to the hospital. If you saw his mugshot, he showed no remorse, whatsoever. He was only worried about getting out of the situation. He really thought he did nothing wrong.

I don't understand how he could have been filled with such anger. So much so that he mutilated a part of me that many women hold precious.

Chapter 7
After The Attack

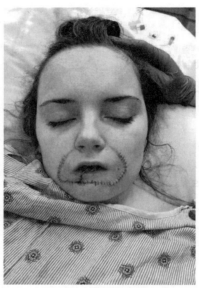

After the First Surgery

I remember waking up, looking up at my nurse and trying to lighten the mood. I made a joke that at least I wouldn't have to dress up for Halloween to scare everyone. I could just go as myself. She smiled, nodded and brought me a mask to cover my face. That was when it hit me — my new reality. What I just woke up from was real; it wasn't just a bad dream. There would never be a day in my life that I would ever wake up again to live my "normal" life. I would have to create a new normal.

The days, weeks and months after the attack were a mix of doubts, confusion, recollection, sadness and anger. I blamed myself for what happened to me. But now I know that I was not at fault. The attack happened because I chose not to get back together with him. I knew he didn't deserve me.

I used to be his property, he thought he owned me. He manipulated me to the point where I lost everyone else in my life. It was all about him. The day that I walked away from the relationship with him was one of the best days of my life. I chose ME. Even if that was the day when he snapped. He realized he lost all control over me and he wasn't going to be successful in another attempt of getting it back. I do believe that was his tipping point. He was always able to get in my head. But not that time — I allowed it no more!

Many people ask me why I stayed if it was that bad. What they don't understand is that sometimes it was very good. Because when he was good, he was loving and caring. I saw a gentle side to him. In the beginning he never pressured me to do something I wasn't ready for. And when he was bad, he became my nightmare. He was a switch that flipped on and off.

I was a naive 17-year-old-girl with my first boyfriend, who was older. My first love and the first one who I thought loved me. Of course I wanted to pursue him and believe the best in him. I thought he could change and become a better person.

I always thought that if I just gave up when it got bad, then it meant I didn't truly love him. But there comes a point where you don't "give up." You get out because you choose YOU. Your mental, emotional and physical wellbeing is more important to protect and value than being with someone who compromises it.

Then the times I did try to get out, it felt worse for me. I was physically and mentally harmed including black eyes, body slamming and shamed in many ways. Finally, I gained the courage to say that it was over and I held firm to my decision.

And, like his family, there were many times that I protected Aaron. But that time he had done something that there was absolutely no excuse for and he needed to face the consequences before the next girl faced something worse than me.

I also experienced many sleepless nights. About a month after the attack, my mom came home to check on me during her lunch break. I was asleep so she just lay next to me. She began having to shake me to wake me up. I was screaming and crying in my sleep because I was having nightmares that my attacker was coming after me again. In fact, I still have them to this day. My biggest fear is that he will get his hands on me again, and next time I may not be here to share my voice.

I used to dream of having a big family and little babies, as many young women do. Afterwards, I wasn't sure if I wanted kids because I felt like bringing them in the world would be putting them in danger. If Aaron could flip like a switch because I refused a kiss, then imagine what he would do if he ran into me or my family again.

On top of the trauma of the attack, I also was dealing with the stress of my grandfather's upcoming trial. It could not have come at a worse time. Luckily, we had the trial delayed so I could heal after the attack. That brought on more trauma. And it didn't end there. I never imagined Aaron would put me through more pain but that is what he did.

A few days after the attack I broke my silence. I posted a Snapchat picture of my face. I was afraid that if I was out and ran into someone I knew, I would be humiliated and break down. By posting a selfie, I could ease back into public. Of course, this started a flood of rumors and assumptions because everyone made up something that they thought happened. A dog attacked me; my ex cut me with a knife. At that point, I was only telling close friends and family.

Meanwhile, Aaron was in jail for 10 days and got out on Halloween. He was out on bond for 362 days doing what he wanted to do, when he wanted, and where he wanted. He was drinking and partying often. He was posing with alcohol in

Recovering with Dog, Ella

Snapchats. I specifically remember one night, he did an Instagram live. There was a girl on it — underage — and they were all drinking at his father's house. The whole family was in the video. Aaron was on at the end. He and the girl were all over each other.

She even posted him lifting up his pant leg and lifting his court-ordered ankle monitor and charger. She said, "Oh she got you good bro, didn't she?" They all broke out in laughter. He showed his ankle monitor as if it was a trophy and he'd won a prize.

The same girl was at my place of work a couple weeks later, drinking, still underage. I walked up to confront her. I asked her if she believed that Aaron wouldn't do anything to her, after what he did to me. She told me she'd known him for eight years and he would never hurt her.

But what women don't think about is that it could happen to them. He could be abusive again.

The monitor they made him wear was both a blessing and a curse for me. I would get calls in the middle of the night from the GPS monitoring system, saying they didn't think I was in danger but they hadn't been able to track him for two hours. And if I saw or heard anything — give them a call. They would always end the call with "have a great night." Click. Midnight, 2 a.m., 4 a.m., 5 a.m. I woke up to all of those calls. And I was supposed to have a good night? Ridiculous!

It was very emotional. It was a roller-coaster ride. One thing after another. From the phone calls to the videos to the posts all over social media. He affected many lives with absolutely no sign of remorse. In the meantime, so many people around me had to switch their lives up — so I could heal.

I also had to make many changes in my life because of him and what he did to me. I could not go back to my home for weeks afterwards. I would panic every time I got a glimpse of the street because the attack was down the street from our front door. It got so bad that we had to sell our home — the first home my mother ever purchased.

I was on so much medication that I couldn't drive for two months. I also feared that I would see him somewhere when he was out on bond. I couldn't, didn't want to go anywhere by myself. I felt frightened to venture out. I sat in my bedroom, constantly scrolling through social media. That led me to compare myself to everyone else on my feeds — which then led to worse thoughts. I felt useless. Meanwhile, we had the police drive by our house frequently to ensure our safety.

When I finally gained the courage to go out, I experienced heads turning constantly to stare at me. I could not even walk out of the house without smothering myself in makeup. People looked at me as a monster. It depleted my already waning confidence and overall quality of life. I tried to act brave. I tried to act like I was ok, but deep down; I just wanted to find the easiest way out of life.

Being a teenage girl is hard to begin with because there are many expectations from society of how you should look. Then imagine how my insecurities skyrocketed once I had a mutilated face, with a scar wrapping from cheek to cheek. I was known as "the girl who had her lip bit off."

My day to day living was affected in other ways too. It took me months to finally open my mouth wide enough to put in a small fork or spoon. I had to use little plastic ones, smaller than baby silverware. I still cannot bite off food, like a sandwich, a burger or pizza. I also had to go through physical therapy by doing exercises to loosen up the scar tissue. The therapists made me eat in front of them so they could observe and see what they could do to help. It was like being a small child learning to do the basics all over again.

The attack also ruined my college plans. I was a month and one-half into my first year of college and had to withdraw. And in doing so, I lost all of my scholarships. I wanted to start back again, but I needed multiple surgeries. So I didn't see how I could. And then my tuition would have to come out of my mother's and my pockets.

Once my story hit the local, then national, and eventually international media, there was a lot of criticism towards my mom for letting me date a 21-year-old. My mom didn't like the age difference, I was 17. She tried to support my relationship with Aaron in the beginning. I was 17 for a month when we began dating and I turned 18 while we were dating. I felt I was old enough to make decisions for myself, or to speak up if something was wrong.

But I didn't speak up. I lost myself. And I lied to my mom, saying I was staying at a friend's house on the weekend. It got to the point where every weekend, I would stay at Aaron's dad's house. I even parked my car at my friend's house and then Aaron would pick me up from there. That way my car was at my friend's house if my mom drove by to check. She didn't want me to stay with him. My mom didn't even know the entirety of it because I didn't let her.

At Aaron's house I will always remember seeing his dad as a raging alcoholic. It was the same behavior I saw in Aaron. I only remember one time when his dad was not drinking while I was over there. That was early in the morning when he just woke up. And that was what we always did when we went over there. Drink. We'd drink until Aaron passed out and I'd go upstairs and go to sleep.

There were several occasions when his stepmom and I would stay downstairs together. She was his father's third wife and in her late 20s. His dad was 50. I remember pouring my heart out to her and telling her what I was going through. I didn't disclose all the details. I did ask her for advice though.

I will never forget what she said to me — she told me to get out while I could.

Or I would end up like her. She said it multiple times. And I did get out.

And Aaron still attacked me.

I guess I shouldn't have been surprised when she turned on me during Aaron's trial in October. I felt it was the biggest stab in the back to see her there to defend him although she didn't actually testify. I know she was his dad's wife — maybe she felt like that was what she needed to do to keep the peace with him. It was a hurtful and an emotional process to get through.

One day at work, I got a call from an investigator connected to the court case telling me not to post anything on social media — making it look like I was happy. It could have an effect in court. I felt very discouraged. Aaron could post whatever he wanted and I couldn't? After I thought about it for a while, I decided I didn't care. He took too much of my life and happiness away. He took my smile. He wasn't going to take anything else from me.

I read this statement to the judge in court during Aaron's trial and later posted it on social media:

I was told to not post anything about being happy or what I was doing, but your honor, Aaron has taken enough of my happiness. I cannot allow him to keep taking it or I will never live the life that I was meant to. No one understands how every day is a struggle to get up and go about my days. And if I sit down and let this defeat me, then he will only get more satisfaction out of what he's done. I just ask that the focus today is on what he has done, and may end up doing if he does not face the consequences. Not how far I have come, or what I have had to do to overcome — what he has done to me.

It was time to take my power back. I posted what I wanted.

I wasn't going to allow him to defeat me.

My impact statement got an unbelievable 70,000 shares on Facebook!

Aaron pleaded guilty in court and was sentenced to 12 years — 85 percent served before being eligible for parole. The prosecutor told the judge that after the attack Aaron was on the phone with his mom, laughing and saying, "She had no bottom lip anyways." I also found out that when he was handcuffed, he had a knife in his pocket. And I wondered — what would he have done with the knife? If he did so much damage with his bare teeth, what could he have done with a weapon? He also was into guns and to this day, I thank God that he didn't have one on him.

Now, I know Aaron never loved me. He loved the idea of me. He loved having someone to turn to when he felt like lashing out. He loved having someone there that he could make feel just as bad or worse when he was down — to make himself feel better. He never loved me for who I was.

I thank God for letting me see the bigger picture — eventually.

I thank God for letting me see another day.

I thank God for giving me the strength I needed.

And I thank God for the people around me, who kept me going.

Chapter 8

The Healing Process

I remember sitting in my room once I left the hospital. Believe it or not, I was thinking about dropping the charges. He was 22 at the time and his life was ruined. I didn't want to ruin his life, he was so young. And then I had to come to the realization that I didn't ruin his life.

He ruined it for himself.

And oftentimes, those who have not experienced domestic abuse have difficulty understanding that even though the abuse took place, the woman can still care and love her abusive partner. It takes time to move beyond that and separate from it.

During those long weeks in bed when I got home, my dog never left my side. She was right there with me. Almost protecting me in a way. She helped me pull myself from him. I became focused on her and was able to mentally pull away from him and eventually cut ties completely.

But that took time.

The physical healing also took time. I knew it wouldn't be easy. The first surgery I had in the hospital right after the attack was a debridement of the lip wound. This cleaned the debris from the wound and the mangled tissue that was left. Then Dr. Boland, my plastic surgeon, performed bilateral Karapandzic flaps technique to reconstruct my lips. Even though the flesh was saved, it could not survive a live reattachment. However, that surgery brought me back to life, so to speak. I had no idea that Dr. Boland was going to be able to restore my face in the ways that he did. It gave me assurance. And waking up and seeing what he had done honestly made me realize that I was going to be okay. I saw no hope before I went under anesthesia. I thought it was going to be horrendous. Of course, I didn't like how I looked but it was better than what I could have ever imagined.

Kayla with Dr. Boland a Week after Surgery

The part that was kind of disappointing was when the surgery was first done. The scar tissue loosened and I had flexibility in my mouth. Over time the scar began to form back and became very thick again, and I've lost flexibility in my mouth. I definitely notice the difference and I have an upcoming surgery in December 2020 so he can work on this once more.

There were several rounds of Kenalog (steroid) injections, profractional laser resurfacing, and hyaluronic acid fillers. There also was a surgical scar revision of the right lower lip with fat grafting to the left lower lip — adding shape and plumping the lip. That felt good. I genuinely felt happy. It was just a fat graft but I felt the most confident. I had a very good "plump" and did not feel so flat faced.

My doctor also tried cadaveric fat transfer at one point but that didn't work all that well. In fact, nothing seems to stay. However with the amount of work and trust that Dr. Boland has put into the process — I keep faith that he will not stop until we both are happy with it. My expectations from the beginning were never high at all — but he has proven himself and his work each time. Although the healing process is very slow, I will always keep faith in him and the next step.

After the attack I was silent for a while, with the exception of close family and friends. I only did a few Snapchats here and there, so people would know that I didn't look like my normal self, if they ran into me somewhere. I didn't want anyone to cause a scene. About eight months after the attack, someone texted me that Aaron had a girlfriend. He was still out on bond. I didn't know what to do. I knew Aaron's way with words and I wanted to protect her. I remember him telling me all his exes were crazy — when it was really him — who was crazy.

So my first post on social media, I wrote to the "next girl." I asked her not to believe the lies and the manipulation. I also advised her not to believe it would get better even if he cried in her arms. I warned her it could escalate from a black eye to a missing lip. I wanted her to see it. I didn't want her to believe what he told her — he thought he did nothing wrong. He played it off as a mistake; he "nibbled" too much.

When I posted that, I suddenly realized how often domestic violence happens. Women opened up to me and shared their stories of abuse. They sent love, support and prayers to me. My post had over 20K shares. That was when I got the idea to create a Facebook Page, *She Rises with Kayla Hayes*. And I shared the impact statement I read to the judge which received 70K shares. My page and awareness grew.

When Aaron pleaded guilty in court, I don't think he had any other choice. There was no way he was getting out of it. Not after the attention I received after my first social media post and the amount of people it reached. There was no way.

Soon after Aaron's mom bashed me on social media saying I was the abusive one and I was the one who caused it. She said I was the one who wanted to meet up. She said I jumped on him to snatch my phone out of his hand. I guess I pretty much expected this reaction. After all, she's his mother. But it was not okay for her to make excuses for his actions.

Moving on to new relationships was difficult after Aaron. I saw everything as a red flag and I found myself comparing everyone to Aaron right off the bat. I felt I saw traits in others that Aaron had too and I distanced myself. I put up a wall. I had no tolerance for any disrespect to me. I feared "Aaron" would happen to me again. I picked up both healthy and unhealthy survivor traits. To this day, I am still trying to push my way out. I feel I always need to have my guard up.

After being in two relationships after Aaron, I realized that I was always in a fight or flight response — from things that I didn't even think were red flags. I was so scared of a possible escalating situation that I took flight. I felt there was no fight left in me. I was diagnosed with anxiety, depression, PTSD, paranoia and I disassociated my mind from my body. I had to learn that one bad boyfriend and grandfather didn't mean all men were bad.

It took a long time but I've changed that now. If I'm in a relationship with someone, I trust him. I refuse to look at a boyfriend's phone. Those habits were hard to change. So was the feeling that I couldn't trust him, thinking an attack could happen again.

To this day, I still have times when I disassociate my mind from my body. I am aware and I know my boundaries now. Before, I could be there physically, but not mentally. I didn't know the fine line between a red flag, and a person being human and messing up. I saw everything as a red flag — I gave a boyfriend three strikes and he was out. That is something I continue to improve upon.

I also had to learn to do my own thing and be me. I had to learn to put my well-being first. I'm not in a relationship as of now. There was a piece of Kayla that died — and I will never get that piece of me back. But there is also a piece of Kayla that was there before the relationship that I can make stronger and even better.

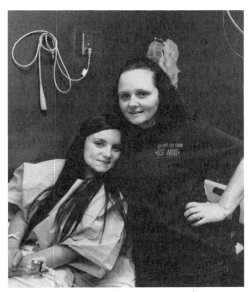

Kayla with Her Mom Before 2nd Surgery

All of my insecurities skyrocketed after the attack. I always felt insecure about my face particularly that my lips were small and Aaron knew that. It was even more difficult being a younger woman, with less confidence. It felt just terrible. I couldn't look in the mirror — I was a ghost in the mirror. I bawled my eyes out. Before the attack I overcame my insecurities by looking into the mirror until I felt happy and could smile. Then I could walk out the door. But that didn't work anymore. I was incapable of smiling at that point.

One of the hardest things was when everyone turned their heads to look at me. Like I was a monster. Or maybe a monkey in a cage at the zoo. They would point their fingers. And based on their facial expressions — I felt inhumane — because of the scar on my face. It defined me. I was known as, "the girl whose lip was bit off." And it defined me for a long time.

Almost three years later I was at work talking with a guy. When we discussed my past he was like, "Oh wow, I heard about your story but I never thought I'd get to meet you. This is insane!" Then he called his wife and said, "Hey honey, you'll never believe...the girl that had her face ripped off by her boyfriend....yeah I'm looking at her now. She's right in front of me."

I know that it's easy for someone to do something simple like that without realizing the impact to the person who is already dealing with so much. I still felt like an animal in a cage. Of course, I'm sure he didn't mean any harm, but it was hard. People didn't see me for me. They saw me for what someone else did to me. I had to find myself through that. I struggled with my identity.

Another time in 2019 I was on a cruise ship walking down the stairs when a little girl said, "Ma'am, what happened to your face?" I was on vacation, enjoying myself. I didn't want to be reminded about the attack or to even think about it. I actually had forgotten about my face. I reminded myself that if I answered the girl correctly, she could take the information with her and she could protect her heart and her body. It just took an ounce more within me to do that. And so I asked her to make sure she only surrounds herself with people who treat her with kindness and respect.

Actually I am finding it easier to forget about my face, until I see a mirror or I see someone else. For a while, it was difficult to be around friends who had beautiful smiles with their white teeth showing. I compared myself and felt "not good enough." I used to feel bothered when kids would point at me. Or if I held a child and they touched the scar on my face. But it doesn't bother me now; I think it's a good conversation starter with kids. They listen to me and what I say. And if I use the right words, they will remember them and they can use them in their own lives.

On the other hand, I felt immense shame and guilt for a long time. I blamed myself. I felt hatred towards myself for believing I "allowed" the behavior to happen. It took time for me to realize that none of it was my fault. As a survivor, this is common. Survivors feel responsibility. How another person's actions became my responsibility, I'm not sure. Maybe it was from manipulation. It was a huge thing that I couldn't get over.

And when I finally did get over what he led me to believe — I knew I was not responsible for his actions.

The most difficult part of healing was the victim blaming that I experienced. People commenting on social media, ... "she was ugly before"... "What did she do to destroy him"... "I bet she won't give him or anyone else lip again"... "She looks like the Joker."

Another difficult part of healing was not knowing who I could trust. Were people just there to get the scoop of what happened, the dirt? So they could turn around and say they knew me? People would come up to me and say, "Hey aren't you that girl? We saw you on the news!" It took me a long time to trust and to let people get close to me and near my face.

I lost a lot of friends. My friends didn't understand that my mind was warped. Showing my face brought anxiety, depression and Post Traumatic Stress Disorder (PTSD). I didn't even know who I was or what I was. I couldn't stand next to my friends after the attack. I felt so insecure. I thought people would label me as the "ugly friend" of the group. I feared the word "ugly." People could say what they want. But ugly to me felt deeper than my outward appearance. That was a lesson I learned very young.

Then things changed. I began to redefine what beauty meant to me. That is when "different" became beautiful to me. I used to look at scars as something ugly and tragic and something that had to be covered up because of imperfection. But scars are not imperfections. They are perfections. They are beautiful. They hold meaning. They say, "I survived." They say you survived. And they can also tell the story of what you overcame.

I went from being an 18-year-old girl that thought she had to live up to the beauty standards in today's world — to finding beauty in being different. Scars, something so horrific and ugly — became something so beautiful and so empowering.

I started researching more about scars and that was when I ran across the quote, "She fought her battles the best she could and she wore her scars as wings." Being a young girl who had a scar wrapping from cheek to cheek — that really hit home to me. When I began letting the words of others get to me and tear me down, I had to realize I was doing the best I could to fight these battles and come out with my head above the water. I decided to use my scars as my wings, as my survival story and even a conversation starter. Rather than thinking people looked at me like I was the monster — they could ask me questions and find hope in something that used to be an imperfection or something weird to them.

There is more. When you think about trauma or the hurt that a scar holds, it is actually quite beautiful. How such things that once seemed to destroy you — did not. They became beautiful and unique marks to show that you survived.

I also experienced a lot of verbal judgments. I had people telling me they were shocked to see me out and about places because, well, that just didn't seem like something I should be doing. Or people telling me that I had my "five seconds of fame and now think I am too good to respond to all the messages I receive."

Some fail to realize that just because someone opens up about what they experienced, it does not make it easy for them. It adds more stress and takes a toll on your healing process at times. I am still only one person and I am just another human being that wants to see good for others.

Sharing my story doesn't make me a saint. I have my bad days, wrong doings, etc. just like the next person. But I also still have feelings and I just turned 22 and believe that I should be able to live a normal life just like any other 22-year-old woman. As much as I love having all of these opportunities to tell my story in the media, through speaking engagements and even this book, I want to be able to live, experience, and have fun outside of just working and sharing my story. People don't see that there has to be that balance.

For a while and even now sometimes, it is hard to find that balance. And that is when I have to take a step back and realize that yes; I will always hold such a strong passion for sharing my story and hearing about others. At the same time, I can't be overcome with that passion. I have to take time for myself. That is when I become my best and am better equipped to be an advocate. I hope others see that I am not "thinking I am better than the next." Each of us is one single person trying to heal from the hurt. We are trying to help save as many people as we can along the way — and we all have to take steps back at times to find balance.

Certainly the healing isn't as easy as some people think. Hearing everyone around me telling me that I am the "strongest person they know" is hard to hear — when deep down there are days that I feel like I am completely crumbling. I don't want to portray myself as someone who just has it all together and hasn't had one hell of an emotional rollercoaster ride along the way. Then, I would be lying. I don't want to give false hope to others that overcoming abuse is a cakewalk. Because it is not.

But if you put in the work, always remember to strive for that better life and believe that you will be okay, then I promise that you can do this and you will get through it. Also, it is extremely important that no matter how far you are in your journey, that you remember that it is okay to have those bad days. It is okay to crumble before picking yourself back up. A bad day doesn't mean a bad life. Just don't stay in the bad day, keep moving forward.

As a brilliant lady once told me, "You can be a masterpiece while having messy pieces at the same time." ~ Alisa Divine

Chapter 9

She Rises & Advocacy

Kayla Receiving the Warrior Recognition Award

While trying to figure out what I needed to do to rise from my abusive relationship and the last attack, the words "she rises" kept floating through my head. I was at a low point — just above the surface of giving up. But I knew there was something that had to be done. Rising from this was the only way out without taking a dark route. I had to truly dig deep. The only thing that could save me was the thought of saving a brother or sister from hitting my dark spot. I wanted to save them from having to experience a tragedy like mine. I realized that I wanted to help people rise from the mess before they got in too deep and ended up like me. I realized that I enjoy life, I love it. No matter what was happening I would find the things worth living for.

I could have easily decided to just trash Aaron's name and his family — but I knew that was not the type of person I was raised to be and not who I wanted to become. I had to come to the realization that this whole situation happened for a reason and there was a purpose for me still being here. I knew I had to stay kind and stay strong.

So this is what I am doing, the best I can. I want to share my message in a positive way. I want to give other men and women out there the strength and power of knowing that there is light in the darkness and that if they keep pursuing it, they can get there as well. Even in the most difficult of circumstances.

And you should expect that the journey won't be easy. Remnants of the abuse will linger in your life for months, even years. In my case, although Aaron was in jail, he still found a way to threaten me. On July 13, 2020, I was at work and a guy started commenting on my Facebook posts, the ones with photos that showed my face after the attack. He said he was in prison with Aaron and he would have killed me if he was there. Aaron told him I paid the lawyers off and he threatened I had "X" amount of days to tell the truth or I would be in deep shit. And I would find out what that deep shit was when the time came. That brought back the fear I thought I already had overcome.

Another reminder is my continuing medical treatment. I am scheduled to have another major surgery to reconstruct my scar — once again, in December 2020. It seems this will be the last surgery but I will continue having lip treatments indefinitely.

So how will I stay focused on my recovery? *She Rises* is one way to share my journey of healing and becoming empowered. The impact of social media is another way. My Facebook page can be used as an outlet and a vehicle to share with others.

For now, my biggest piece of advice for a survivor of teen dating violence (TDV), domestic violence (DV), and sexual abuse (SA) is to use what you have gone through as the strength to keep pushing and find a bigger purpose in it. I want others to know that the person that abused them does not deserve to hold back or tear down any of their happiness any longer. When I feel like I am hitting a low point in my healing journey, I always like to remind myself that Aaron took a year (plus) of my happiness and he tried to take my smile forever. But then I remember that he is no longer in control of either one and he never deserves to be again.

I also surround myself with people who support me and who I can support as well. I've taken a step back lately to evaluate the people and the things in my life. I want to focus on what is going to benefit my future.

Without a doubt, Break the Silence — the survivor sister family — has changed my life. I feel like I really relate to them. I can talk to my mom and my friends, but they don't fully understand. They've never gone through it. And unless you've gone through something similar, you have no idea how it feels. I highly recommend finding people you can relate to.

At first I tried to hold all of my feelings in and I felt like I was a tornado. But I sought help. I've been put on medication, had counseling and even taken steps back at times. However, I found that it has been very therapeutic to write and speak about my story.

I have told my story through several different outlets. I have been blessed with the opportunity of sharing it on news programs in my hometown. I also have shared it with a national audience through a short clip on *Inside Edition*, an online interview for *Cosmopolitan* Magazine, a podcast for *Medialounge Chicago* and several others, an interview for *Fox Carolina*, a chapter in the book *#She Wins,* I've spoken through Zoom conferences, through videography and more. I have made speeches at various clubs, organizations and schools and have been presented with awards for my courage. All have brought much more support than I could have ever imagined.

I remember the first speaking engagement I did was in front of a room full of strangers. Not many of them said anything to me when I originally walked through the door but by the time I left they were spreading an outpouring of love and offering connections where I could share my message.

Most of the time the speaking engagements turned out like the first one but once in a while there was some backlash. Members of the audience tried to harass and stalk me. Some even tried to bribe me to hush me up. The backlash is shitty but if it saves another life then it is worth it. I made up my mind that I will never be silenced. I will be screaming from the rooftops just to save one girl from a living hell — even if it takes my last breathe to do so.

I also find that writing about my story as well as listening to other women tells theirs is extremely helpful. I met many people on Facebook and Instagram. So many women poured their hearts out on posts. That helped me to see that abuse is all around us. It's time to step up and be there for each other and share our stories, love each other. Spread love around.

I like to think that my Facebook Page *She Rises* is a source of safety and knowledge for victims and survivors. I want them to know that they are not alone. *She Rises* currently consists of a "family" of almost 50K. That's 50,000 people who could save someone's life by just sharing one post. Knowing that what I post along with others sharing it helps make a difference.

That is why a support system is essential. As much as we want to tell ourselves that we can do this alone — having a support system is a major comfort. Surrounding yourself with people that can truly understand you and understand what you have gone through is going to help you overcome and know that you are not alone. Knowing that you are not the only one around that has suffered from abuse is like taking a burden off of your shoulders. It allows you to see that you too, can come through this as others have.

Finally, the biggest thing that inspires me to keep going is those who have lost their voice or not yet found it. Had the circumstances just been slightly different, that could have been me? After getting hurt and having other women share their stories with me — I realize how much of an impact I can make by just sharing a few simple words.

Luckily, by telling my story and listening to others tell theirs, I know that my life is going to be okay again.

Part II:
A Guide to Overcoming Abuse

How to Use This Section

This section of the book is meant to be used as a guide. A guide for women who have experienced abuse and/or hardships in any form. In addition, it can be used as a tool for prevention of abusive relationships. You can use this guide for yourself. And maybe there is someone you know who could greatly benefit from reading this. Each of us can only take responsibility for our own personal healing and overcoming. And when you take responsibility to heal yourself, you begin turning pain into power, regardless of who was at fault.

If you know someone who can benefit from reading this — a simple way to approach it is by sharing your copy or purchasing another and saying, "I've found helpful information in here and maybe you will find it helpful as well."

And that's all that is necessary. The rest is in her hands, it's her responsibility.

As you read through this next section, you will learn the five steps to overcoming. Throughout the steps, you will find journal prompts. I want to share the power of journaling with you. One way to heal your life is through the process of journaling. You can look back through your journal and see your progress. I journal daily, every morning. In addition, I journal when I am faced with a challenging situation or when I want clarity on a subject. And I always get the answers I am looking for. I will tell you, journaling has allowed me to heal my hurts and gain more personal power over my life than anything else I've experienced.

At this time, I highly suggest grabbing a journal of your choice. Some options are a spiral notebook, a fancy leather journal or a Google Doc/Google Folder on your computer. Utilize the journal prompts in preparation of your own journey to healing and freedom from your past.

A few tips for journaling:

- Write as a release, or a brain dump, letting out what you've been holding in.
- Do not worry about grammar, punctuation or spelling — just write.
- If you want to correct the above, go through it a couple days later and make the changes.
- When journaling, nothing is wrong and everything is right.
- If you can't think of what to write at first, write "I don't know what to write" and simply let more thoughts surface and flow onto your paper or document. The more you do it, the more natural it becomes.
- Use journaling as a record of your progress and celebrate all your wins, big and small.
- Journaling in the morning when your mind is fresh and you have the least amount of resistance is most effective, whether you can take 15 minutes or 30 minutes.

Now — onward and upward — you can overcome!

Chapter 1

Heal What Hurts

There are many reasons why people do not heal their hurts. They may not be aware that the hurts are still there. Especially if the hurt happened years ago, they may think they "got over it" or "forgot about it." And there's a probability that it shows up as a constant struggle without understanding the source. As in — life feels hard. It feels unfair. You move from one struggle to another and then another. When you think the struggle ends, another shows up shortly after. You just want a break! And you ask, when is it going to be my turn for something good to happen? I am a good person! I try so hard! I want more. I deserve better. Does this sound familiar?

We want to heal our hurts because when we don't, the hurts leak into our daily lives. And without the awareness that it is happening, we stay stuck. Or maybe we think that we healed it but the heal was not complete — so it comes back, the wound reopens. It can feel like a cancer that eats away at our wellbeing. Only, unlike cancer, it doesn't show up through labs and x-rays, it shows up in our relationships, and in our confidence and in our mindset. It shows up in the amount of money we earn or have in our bank account — or that which we do not have. It shows up in all the ways that are invisible. It's dangerous that way because it's not visible and we often keep it a secret. Never really reaching our full potential, never shining our lights as brightly as they can shine.

We want to heal our hurts because we know — there is more to life than the struggle. We know there is more we are meant to do, or people we can help. We just know it. But we don't know how to change it. Keep reading, because now you will find out.

I coached a woman who struggled with self-worth but it showed up in her finances. She accumulated a large amount of debt, felt guilty about it, and couldn't seem to ever "get ahead." For years she thought she had a money problem, only to finally discover she didn't believe she was worthy of having a full life in all areas, money included. Her thermostat was set to a low level of happiness. And when the thermostat began to rise, she had to bring it back down because she wasn't comfortable with too much happiness. She did this without being aware that she was doing it. It was a confidence and self-worth struggle that went back to her teenage years. It was not even a money problem. The struggle became a way of life and she held onto hurts she wasn't aware of. The struggle was a comfort, the struggle was familiar. It was all she knew. And sometimes people stay there forever. In a constant state of struggle. But she didn't. She used the tools and resources to heal that we are sharing in this book.

Now, you can make the choice to stop the struggle and claim a life you are excited to live!

Sometimes, our hurts go back to something that happened in childhood, as you read here in the example of Kayla and the sexual abuse she endured. Maybe your hurt is similar. Or maybe it is different, such as a fear of not feeling accepted, or wanted or loved. The list of circumstances is endless. When the hurts go unhealed, or ignored — aka — "I'm tough and I'll just get over it," or they are only addressed at the surface level, they can come back. And without the knowledge and awareness to address them, they continue to affect daily living. Using Kayla's belief she adopted as a child — that she had to cower down to men because that's what happened with her grandfather — led her to believe she had to do that with Aaron as well. She was left feeling she didn't have any choices. She felt powerless. She moved from the struggle with her grandfather to the struggle with her boyfriend.

Our hurts are stories in our mind that have been playing on repeat. We can be a masterpiece and have messy pieces at the same time. And we get to rewrite our stories and become the masters of our minds. Now, you can get off the emotional rollercoaster and claim the life you really want! It's time to let go of what's been holding you back and walk on the path of freedom and a new way of living.

How To Heal What Hurts:

1. Be Intentional

   Make a commitment to take the time and heal. This is a choice.

   Begin by making a list of the hardships you've experienced. Examples to begin your list are below and certainly not limited to the list. The hardships could have been brought on by yourself and also by others. List them all on your journal or Google Doc. Do a brain dump to get them out of your mind. This is the first step to heal your life.

   This can take some time and you may want to spend an hour, a few days or a week writing your list. Go back as far as you can remember. Some are smaller and some are more significant. Write them all. Some are things people say or do or don't do, or don't say. There could be things you've said, didn't say, have done, or have not done. Write down everything that comes up for you. There is nothing too small to list. Allow yourself some space as well, to let it all bubble to the surface. You may remember a few days into this about something you want to add to your list. Go back and add it in.

2. Identify the Hurts:

   Hurt feelings from others about...

Feeling worthless because...

Feeling not enough when...

Being let down by....because...

Embarrassment over...

Abuse from others: sexual, emotional, financial, mental, physical...

Your own bad choices of...

Your own bad thoughts about....

Self-harm...

Betrayal by...

Not being believed about...

Feeling invisible to...

Abandonment by...

Disappointment from...

Guilt for...

Shame over...

There's a high probability that when you make the commitment and take the time to do this exercise, you will recall memories and events that you didn't even realize you were holding onto and making space for in your mind. That is why this exercise is important to do. There is no longer room for those memories to rent space, time, or energy in your mind. The first step to changing your thoughts is being aware of them.

3. Break the Bonds

Now that you have your list, it is time to break the bonds with your hurts. Here are some exercises to "break up" with your hurts. If you think of additional hurts after you begin this step, add them to your list and repeat this process for the most recent additions. I recommend reading through all the exercises and choosing what you feel most drawn to. Some hurts may have more impact than others and you may prefer one exercise over another.

Writing Exercise #1

- Write a letter to yourself. Set aside some time to do this. There are four paragraphs to write. In the first paragraph you want to write all the dirt that happened either in a specific relationship or throughout your life. Go through all the bad stuff.
- The second paragraph is going to be focused on how you felt about the "dirt." Describe the effects it had on you, the problems that arose from it and the emotions you felt.
- The third paragraph is focused on how you are changing it. List the steps you are taking to get the reins to your life back, own your personal power, and take full responsibility for your life from this moment on. Are you getting help from someone with a similar experience? Are you working with someone such as a coach or a therapist? Are you taking care of your body, mind and soul? Are you choosing only healthy relationships from this point on? Are you drawing boundaries? What are you doing differently? Who are you being? How does it feel? In order to create new experiences, different from the ones that did not work out for you before, you want to create new beliefs and new actions to reflect the life you desire.
- The fourth paragraph is a glimpse into your life a few years from now. How is it different? What have you been able to accomplish? Are you in a relationship? If so, what does it look and feel like? In what ways are you successful? How does it feel? Give yourself permission to think big here, to dream and state what you really want from life.

- The next step of this writing process is to fold up your letter, put it into an envelope, address it to yourself, put a stamp on it and mail it. You are also going to set aside a large manila envelope. When you receive this letter in the mail it will have the date marked. Yes, your postmaster may wonder why there is a letter to you, from you — let him/her wonder. Put it into the manila envelope. When you experience something challenging, or you miss the person who was toxic, because we know that there were some good times with the bad time, take out your letter. Read it. Recall the dirt. Recall how you felt. Recall what you are doing and who you are being to change your life and your outcomes. And recall what you are working towards, what your life is going to look and feel like as you consistently take steps forward. It will give you the strength and the courage to keep moving on your higher path to healing and freedom.

- When I divorced eight years ago, I did this exact exercise. At the time, I felt a lot of guilt for leaving him even though I knew it was the best choice. I felt guilt because we had five children together and their lives were changing. I had even left multiple times before the final time. And I always went back. But not that time. That letter alone saved me from going back once again. When times were difficult through the divorce and with the custody arrangement of our children and beyond, I took the letter out of the manila envelope multiple times and read it. I remembered why I was doing what I was doing. I remembered why it was the right choice for me to leave. That lasted for a couple years. Each time I took the letter out and read it, I sent it back to myself in the mail, so all the times are postmarked with dates. And I saved the envelopes in the large manila envelope. One day as my kids become adults, if they ask me why I left their father, I am going to take out the letter. If they ask me why I have all the opened envelopes addressed to myself, I will tell them that is how many times I questioned myself if I was doing the right thing. And each time I read my letter I knew that I did indeed make the best decision for everyone involved.

- Isn't that powerful? It works. Use my example as evidence that it will work for you too. You may need to make adjustments, such as finding an alternative place to mail your letter if you are living with the person you are writing about, such as a parent's house or a friend's. And let them know ahead of time that they may see a letter for you. Ask them to keep it in a safe place until you can pick it up. You can also choose an alternative name in the return address such as a pet or fictitious character if you feel more comfortable doing that.

Writing Exercise #2

Write a letter to the person who hurt you. Use the four paragraphs in the exercise above, writing directly to that person. Tell them what they did, how you felt, what you are doing to change your life and tell them about the best version of YOU. Tell them they no longer hold power over you — you are taking your power back. Then take the letter and rip it up into tiny pieces, feeling the power that person once had over you disintegrating. OR take your letter and burn it in your fireplace or in an outdoor campfire. Create an experience around it. Watch the power the person once had over you go up in flames. Then celebrate. Celebrate your decision to choose you, to heal, and to overcome. We want to celebrate all our wins, big and small.

- Rewrite Your Story

    Kayla took on the story that she had to cower down to men and do what they said. And rightfully so, she was forced into sexual acts as a child by her grandfather, a person she loved and trusted. Cowering down to men and having to do what they said was a story, a belief that became real for her. That story can be rewritten to one that is empowering and serves her. With the awareness, she changed the story to — I am empowered in the presence of men and I have the ability to make my own choices. Each of you also holds the power to change your beliefs to ones that are empowering and serve you.

While in the process of finishing this book, Kayla turned her new story into action. She received death threats from a guy who was in prison with her ex-boyfriend. Kayla was strong in her boundaries and that man crossed them. She pressed charges against him and he was arrested. He awaits a trial and sentencing. Kayla no longer believed she had to cower down to men. She took her power back and made the choice to stand up and protect herself while holding him accountable. Even though it was not an easy decision for Kayla to make, she had refused to let another person hold power over her again. In fact, the first time she went to the police department, she was sent home — but she did not give up. She pressed on, found someone who helped her and she rewrote her story.

The first step is to heal the hurt, become aware of the story that no longer serves you. Then change the story to a new belief that is empowering. In Kayla's example she said — cowering down to men and having to do what they say is not my story. I don't believe that. I want to change that story and stand up to anyone who tries to cross my boundaries. That is my grandfather's belief — that I had to cower down and do what he said. And it's no longer my belief. I have a new belief, a new story to write for my life.

- Forgiveness

We've all had scenarios or people that have done us wrong, hurt us, let us down, or maybe we are hard on ourselves for those things or we are hard on our parents for what they did or didn't do for us. Thinking about these events or people can hinder our mindset and throw us off track. Forgiveness is not saying what someone did was acceptable. Nor is it about letting them "off the hook." It's a decision you make to release the negative energy and the disempowerment you've felt. It's not about the other person. It is making peace with yourself that you did the best you could at the time with the resources you had. And then shift your focus to what you can do in your life right now with the resources you have right now.

- **HO'OPONOPONO**

This is an ancient Hawaiian practice known to clear negativity from the minds of those who practice it. Dr. Ihaleakala Hew Len, was a psychotherapist who used this to cure an entire ward of criminally insane patients without meeting them or spending time with them. You can read more about this story by doing a Google search on it. There also are YouTube videos that guide you through the steps so you can practice this too.

There are multiple variations of using these four steps and find the one that fits for you. You can also create your own ritual using the four steps. The premise is to use this tool to clear limiting beliefs and clear negativity from your mind. The steps are four phrases:

1. I love you
2. I'm sorry
3. Please forgive me
4. Thank you

Some use this as a meditation, repeating these four phrases over in a quiet space and location in order to connect with God, the universe, or a higher power. And here, your focus is on reconnecting to your higher being; to the one you lost connection with, to remember who you are again by removing what's been holding you back.

You can take it a step further and attach meaning to the four phrases. For example, Kayla can say I'm sorry to herself for believing the story her grandfather passed on to her that she had to cower down to men and do what they say. I'm sorry that was what I knew and what I thought I had to do. Then "I love you," I love you Kayla for pushing through to help others from what you experienced. Now, I know how to stand up for myself, draw boundaries and love myself. "Please forgive me" for what I didn't know at the time, I was a child. "Thank you" for the awareness I have about it now and the know-how to get rid of the old story and write a new one.

- Cut the Cords

    There are invisible energetic cords between you and those who you share relationships with. Cords can transmit different types of energies. The practice of cutting the cords allows you to break the bond of negative energy with people you are connected to by the cord. You can release the negative bond and heal your energy through this process. Kayla would go through the cord cutting process with her grandfather and again with Aaron. And from the list you have created, you may have more people to take through this process. If there are multiple people, practice this exercise over a few days or a few weeks until you get through your list. Here is an option and you can search more cord-cutting rituals on YouTube.

    https://gabbybernstein.com/cut-the-cord/ and https://gabbybernstein.com/get-closure-past-relationship/

- Create a Shield

    Imagine being a room with the person who did you wrong. All of the "stuff" between you is in the room as well. Everything that made you feel less than, unworthy, unvalued and unloved. And then you put on your shield of armor. What does it look like? Is it made of steel or titanium or even diamonds that cannot be penetrated? The person who hurt you hurls a familiar phrase or a put down and you watch — you watch it bounce directly off your shield and boomerang right back to him. And you smile because that person can no longer hurt you, or break through your shield.

- Work With Someone

    Find a person who has experienced sexual assault or domestic abuse and has overcome it. Ask to work with that person so they can give you support to reach the stage of overcoming. What I see happening is that women think they have dealt with their situation and then something triggers the flood of negativity and brings back all the emotions as if the event happened yesterday. And what we need is a maintenance plan to handle the triggers and remind us of our progress. It's helpful to have a coach, mentor, or therapist to remind us what to do, think and how to be when we hit bumps on the road so we can get back on track quickly and easily time after time. That is the key to overcoming.

The theme of this section you just read is to break the bonds to what or who has hurt us. This works. I've experienced my own breakthroughs and so has Kayla from doing these exercises.

I want to add that you may want to choose one or more of these exercises to repeat in four months or six months. Add it into your calendar now. Just like when you buy a vehicle and you maintain it by getting oil changes, going through the car wash and rotating the tires for it to run at its best. Scheduling maintenance on your healing and overcoming also ensures it will last at the same quality as when you started it. Also, add any new events or people you want to break bonds with that has occurred more recently. Make it your priority to take responsibility to heal what hurts you. It is up to you. And it is something within your control. Choose to be intentional. When you do this, you free space in your mind, you release distractions, you release the struggle, and then you have the time and energy to focus on what you really want for your life. You move from the mentality of a victim to taking control over your life and utilizing your personal power.

Chapter 2

Identify What You Want

When you know what you don't want, use that to identify what you do want. You know you don't want to be sexually assaulted or be in an abusive relationship. You've had the opportunity and gained the know-how to clear out what hasn't worked for you. So what do you want in place of that? Do you want to be in a healthy relationship where your partner respects you? Do you want to make choices for yourself and feel valued as an individual?

This is where we want to get really clear on what we want. When we don't have clarity and identify what we want, it is a problem because we often settle for what is in front of us. And it could be the wrong fit, such as a toxic relationship or a job that is draining and unfulfilling. It could also be limiting, as not using our full potential or capability. Be intentional and create your life and your life experiences. Yes — you can do that.

And yes — it's really fun to do once you know how.

At this point, you have a clear awareness of what you don't want. And I want you to get even more clear and define your boundaries. What are you not willing to compromise on? What line do others not get to cross with you — physically, mentally, emotionally? What about your time? Are you unavailable for drama? Do you set limits on your time so you get enough sleep? And so you have time for yourself? When we place limits on what we accept into our lives, our bodies and our minds, we feel in control of our lives and are empowered. When we allow others to cross our boundaries — whether we realize we have them or not, we feel disempowered and feel we have lost control. If you are not drawing clearly defined boundaries, it is likely that your power and your energy leak out. This shows up as feeling drained and without energy and zest for life. Now you can change it.

Writing Exercise #3

Now it is time to journal and write out what you do not want, or the boundaries you draw in all areas of your life: relationships, health, mindset, work and finances, and your personal development.

In my relationships, I will not tolerate the following behaviors….

And if those behaviors occur, I know I can……

When another person chooses to cross a boundary I've set, I know that it is in my power to….

If XYZ occurs in a relationship, I see it as toxic behavior and I know it's time to end it….

As part of my health and energy routine, I do not allow…

I do not allow others to interfere with my sleep or time for myself or….

Writing Exercise #4

Now that you've created clarity on what you don't want and have defined your boundaries, you are ready to get clarity on what you do want. This is the fun part. I want you to think big, to feel expansive, to dream. You don't have to know "how" this will happen. The purpose of this exercise is to expand your thinking and expand your focus of what's possible. The only limits to who you can be, what you can have, and what you do in your life — are the limits you place on yourself. As you walk this path, the "how" will appear.

In your journal write: If I could have it all my way....

Again, this is a prompt you want to spend time on. You can do an initial journaling and then as you think of additional pieces to add to your list throughout the following week or month, add them to your journal.

If you could have it all your way, what does your life look like and feel like in the areas of health and wellbeing? What is your mindset practice? What kinds of food do you eat? Do you prepare them or are they prepared for you, or a combination? Do you work out or exercise or walk on a regular basis? Do you spend time investing in yourself by getting enough sleep? How do you choose to dress when you are at work, or at home, or out on the town? Do you choose to spend time on your appearance? Whether you want to wear makeup and get your hair styled or not is your choice. What feels good to you?

Your power is in how you feel about the choices you make. The goal is to be in alignment with your choices in all the above areas of life. Are you happy with how you show up each day? Each hour? If yes, then keep doing what you are doing. If no, then now is the time to identify what you want and make moves to be in alignment with what you want. Maybe you make big shifts or you start with a small shift towards what you want — either way, take one step forward.

If you could have it all your way, what does your life look like and feel like in the area of relationships? Are they healthy? Do they feel good? Are your wants and needs respected and valued? Do you cut out toxic relationships without feeling guilty, even if they are intimate or familial relationships? Do you spend time with friends who energize you?

If you could have it all your way, what does your work and career look and feel like?

If you could have it all your way, what do your finances look like and feel like?

If you could have it all your way, what does your self-development look like and feel life? Do you read? Or travel? Or have meaningful conversations with friends you trust? Do you invest your time or money in ways that inspire you, lift you up and bring you feelings of expansiveness?

What are your highest values? What is most important to you?

What are your top five priorities?

Writing Exercise #5

In your journal, write about your ideal life, five years from now. If you can have it all your way, what does your life look like in all five areas — relationships, health, mindset, work and finances, and your personal development. Who are you? Who is that woman? What choices do you make? What conversations do you have? What kind of work do you do? Where do you go? Who do you spend time with?

When you achieve this level of clarity on what you don't want in life, what your boundaries are, what you do want in life, and who you want to become, you are paving your way to massive success. Your days flow with more ease. You make decisions with more ease as you have built a template for yourself. If you are faced with a choice, one way to decide is to ask, what would the woman I am becoming decide? Would she say yes, or would she say no? Where would she take action? What boundaries does she draw? Use these journal prompts and your discoveries as a compass for your life. Choose beliefs and actions that are in alignment with the woman you are becoming.

-- To take this another step further, you can make a vision board with what you desire to create in your life. You can do this with photos, print images you find online, or in magazines. You also can create a dream board on Pinterest and when you combine your thoughts with visuals, it creates a bigger impact. Really channel who the woman is that you choose to be.

-- Another option is to find a coach or a mentor to help you through this process with encouragement and accountability to see it through.

-- An additional option is to share this with a friend or a group and encourage each other through the process. Share your ideas, your thoughts, get feedback, dream big, and then remind each other on days that feel challenging of who you are and where you are going. The world needs more women who encourage and lift each other up. The world needs women who celebrate each other's success and cheer each other on!

-- To take that yet another step further, create your own mastermind or group where you meet in person or over Zoom once a week to help each other draw boundaries, decide what you want in all areas of life and then follow through with action steps in the direction of your vision.

Chapter 3

Master Your Mindset

We have cleared what didn't serve us and we continue building what does serve us. A regular mindset practice is the base, a building block to build confidence and turn pain into power for your life. There's not a wrong way to do this — unless you don't do it. What I mean is that everyone has their own mindset fit and it may take time to figure out what fit works for you, especially if this is new to you. So I want you to get comfortable with the process of developing a mindset and be okay with changing it over time to adjust to your needs. As you move to new levels in your life, your mindset will also require a leveling up.

I've had many different mindset processes and have changed and adjusted them. I like what I have currently and I may change it later on as I grow and change. I know this is an ongoing practice that will last as long as I live. I will tell you that I do my mindset practice every day. And I've discovered that it works best in the morning as soon as I wake up. This is the most effective time because our thoughts have cleared from sleeping, we have renewed energy. Throughout the day we get distractions from emails, phone calls, work, kids, friends and family. They add up. When we can start each day with an extra barrier — a mindset practice — it helps us to be better versions of ourselves. It helps us to be better equipped to handle challenges that arise.

I want you to create a mindset practice to nurture the trifecta of Body—Mind—Soul. You are caring for the trifecta, which is powerful and underestimated at the same time. Here are ideas for you to begin building and please incorporate other options you discover that are a fit for you. The fit is the magic pill. Begin with the practices that feel the most exciting to you. I used to spend up to a couple hours per day on my mindset alone. I was a personal development junkie. Nowadays, I spend about 30 to 60 minutes, right when I wake up. And I practice it over coffee and it has become my favorite part of the day. I light a candle, listen to an audio and I journal my intentions for the day along with visualizing and channeling the woman I am being to guide me through the day. I feel more equipped to handle challenges as they arise. I make choices to be aligned with the woman I am becoming, she's always evolving.

1. Body

    Eating healthy meals and snacks.

    Consciously choosing what you put into your body.

    Getting enough sleep.

    Yoga or exercise regularly.

    Creative dance.

    Taking a shower or bath daily. Developing rituals to feel your best.

    Being intentional and feeling good about what you wear, your appearance.

    Getting a massage.

    Getting nails done.

    Getting regular haircuts or highlights or color.

    I don't like to exercise but when I have a regular routine, I feel healthy. So I started a couple years ago with a minimum of 10 minutes on the treadmill, with my favorite playlist on Spotify.

That was something I could do with the least amount of resistance, meaning it was the easiest form of exercise I could tolerate. I also used to aim for 3-4 times per week. What I found that is actually easier is to make it a goal for seven days a week. I don't think about it, I don't wonder if it's the right day, it is just a habit. Now, I've upgraded to a 15 minute walk outside daily, with my favorite playlist. I don't know how far I go but it doesn't matter to me. I am moving my body, I feel good doing it and I am more connected to nature. Make your exercise routine a no brainer. Make it so easy you can't not do it!

2. Mind

   Gratitude, there is power in being thankful for what you have — even if it's not everything you want yet...or if you're not where you want to be yet. I practice this before I get out of bed in the morning. Maybe it's prayer or a mental list. That one small act of five minutes shifts the way I start my day. I carve time for myself each day to read or listen to something I want to learn about, to focus on what I'm doing for the day. I journal when I want to figure out something or make a decision. I can answer my own questions through journaling. Work with someone who can help you to get where you want to be, such as a coach or a therapist. Meditations are helpful to quiet your mind and reduce stress, find those that are a good fit for you. Listen to an audio or podcast in an area you want knowledge in. Also choose affirmations that fit the goals you want for your life. Begin with one affirmation for each area you want to improve. Recite it with emotion, and create one action step to do now to move it in the right direction.

3. Soul

   What is good for your soul? Make a list. Is it listening to music? Perhaps it's spending time in meditation or prayer. Reading a book. Participating in art or creative expression. Watching a feel-good movie. Going for a walk in nature, or visiting the ocean. Petting your dog or cat. Recall how Kayla's dog helped her get through the breakup and the healing process. Quiet time alone or time spent with close friends. Traveling for adventure. Taking a relaxing bath with salts and candles. This is something that makes you feel alive. This is something that fills your cup and energizes you.

4. Provisions

    Provisions are what you have in your toolbox when you have a difficult day. Think of provisions as an extra layer of protection when you need it. The self-care above is to pick and choose from daily. You want to have provisions in place to prevent yourself from "losing it." It's like self-care on steroids. An example for me is: going to bed early, making my favorite dinner, taking some time alone to read or listen to something I find inspirational, enjoying a piece of fancy chocolate. Plan for this. Have these things nearby where you can call upon them when you need the extra boost. And have more provisions than what you need in case one doesn't work out or can't fit the time schedule. Provisions are not something you implement when you have time. You put provisions into place when you need them and all other activities go to the back burner. This is not being indulgent. This is taking care of yourself, just like you would go to the doctor for a broken bone. Make it a necessity to care for your mind, body and soul.

5. Create More Joy

    This is a quick but intentional act you can do each day, simply by asking yourself, "What can I do to create more joy today?" Think about what brings you joy. I'm talking about the little things we can do. There is power in simple pleasures. Maybe it's something different each day. Going out or making yourself a special lunch, a celebration with a glass of champagne for an accomplishment, buying the person's coffee behind you in the Starbucks line. Smiling at someone, making eye contact and saying "hi" as you walk by. Giving yourself one-half hour to do something nice for yourself in the evening. Wearing red lipstick. Wearing the fancy dress for no special reason or event. Putting new sheets on your bed. Calling or texting someone and telling them you are thinking of them and are happy they're in your life. Lighting candles or adding your favorite scents more abundantly into your days.

6. Take Responsibility & Recognize Personal Power

    We can only control ourselves. We cannot control other people; we can only control how we respond to them. When we understand this, we know where our power lies — within ourselves. Make more choices for your life and it will become more natural to you. It becomes easier to say no, to draw boundaries, to choose your well-being. Note that when you are not making a choice for yourself — such as if you are asked if you want corn or green beans with dinner and you say, "I don't care" — someone else is making a choice for you. Now that might seem ok in this example, however choices change with life and become much more complicated. What if someone asks you to have sex? "I don't care" takes on a new perspective now, right? And if you'd had practice saying yes or no based on making smaller decisions for yourself, you are equipped to handle larger decisions. You say "no" to what you don't want. And you then choose what you do want. If you are a parent, begin giving your children more opportunities to make choices and learn the art of decision making. It's empowering.

Chapter 4

Build Confidence

As we begin discussing how to raise our confidence, we also want to look at the blocks that prevent us from feeling and being confident. When we can identify what stops our confidence, we can dissolve those thoughts and actions, replacing them with better thoughts and actions to embody who we really are. Then we build our confidence, brick by brick, one small shift to the next shift. And that is where the magic is!

1. The Comparison Confidence Block

    Comparing ourselves to other people in ways of looks, accomplishments, status, relationships, money and personal belongings leads to jealous feelings. It is one of the biggest blocks to confidence. Why? Because the focus is on someone else or something else and that is disempowering. We can only control one person, ourselves. That's where your power is. Within you. If you focus on someone else or something else, you focus on what you cannot control. Shift your focus to what you can control — you.

    Dissolving The Comparison Block: Although comparison and jealousy may be first responses, you can shift them and use them as a tool to build your confidence. First, identify what it is you are comparing. Take notes on your phone, journal or Google Doc. Use the jealous feeling as a way to identify what it is that you want. Is it her outfit or style? Is it that she goes after what she wants and is successful? Is it that she has an unwavering belief in herself? Is it the vacations she takes? Identify exactly what it is that triggers the jealous feeling. Every woman has compared or felt jealous at a point in her life! So let's look at how we can shift those thoughts and feelings.

Once you identify what it is you desire, then do it, be it and go get it. If it's her outfit, how can you create a style that you absolutely love with minimal expense or effort? Is it that she goes after what she wants and is successful? Then create a new goal for yourself in the direction of your dreams. Is it that her life seems easy? Then create more ease for yourself by clearing out what doesn't work for you. Is it that she has an unwavering belief in herself? Then make a plan and take the action steps. Make the decision to go after what you want. Drastic changes are not necessary. Start from where you are, with what you have. Or make the decision that you don't want to put in the time and effort to create new levels in your life. Both ways work. Which one feels more exciting to you?

Explore and discover what it is that you want and make a commitment to do it, one step at a time. Trust yourself. Build yourself up, find your success and celebrate your wins, big and small. Focus on your strengths. Practice your mindset daily or multiple times per day. Build a team of women around you who support you and want you to succeed. The best investment you will ever make is the investment in yourself. Whether it is through time, money, self-care, education and energy — investing in yourself yields the most valuable return on investment.

2. The Playing Small Block

This also shows up as living in survival mode or struggling or victim mode. It can include not knowing how to take responsibility for your happiness. Or saying you can't be happy because someone took it from you. Playing small could be not going after the job you want or the car or the house you want because others might think you are selfish. Or only taking time for yourself if everyone else's needs are met first, then you get the time that is left. And if there is nothing left — well there's always tomorrow. Tomorrow arrives and there is still no extra time. Because being selfish is "bad." It's better to focus on other people, what they want, what is best for your kids and your family and you get what is left over. Because that's what good moms do, they eat the leftovers. They get the leftover time. The leftover money. The leftover energy. That's what "good girls" are taught to do. They don't make other people jealous by being too pretty, too wealthy, or too smart. These thoughts serve no one.

And what does playing small create? A lot of women and girls who can't fully be who they are because they've been taught not to be "too much." Again these are stories that are made up and believed over time. And we can change our stories and beliefs to something that feels better and serves our well-being and success.

Dissolving the Playing Small Block: Go back to what you identified you wanted for your life. Go back to the "If I could have it all my way" journal prompt where you wrote about what you want your life to look like in the areas of: Health & Wellness, Your Career, Self-Development, Finances, Relationships, Family, Friends and Free Time. Take time to write out a section for each if you didn't already. This is not the time or place to play small. You don't have to write what is reasonable or what you can justify getting, not to make others upset. Harness the possibilities.

Use this as a dream board or vision board. So don't just write what you think you might be able to have, write what you would really love to have. Even if you don't know how it will happen. When you play big, when you play the game of life with confidence — everything and everyone around you shows up differently. Things that used to bother you, fall away. Things you used to worry about, you forget about. People show up. Resources show up. When you know, when you really know you are worth putting the time and effort into yourself, other people around you rise to the occasion. They notice.

And if you are not yet in the place of "knowing" you are worth having, doing and being who you want — then borrow my belief that you are. If you are reading this book — you are worthy of having the very best in life. Be open to receiving it all.

3. The Body Language Block

The way we sit and the way we stand, if we close down and make ourselves smaller, it is associated with feeling less powerful, or lacking confidence. Or it can be associated with confidence and power if we change our posture to expand and make our bodies larger and more open.

Dissolving The Body Language Block: Simple shifts in our body language can lift our confidence. The *Ted Talk* link below by Amy Cuddy explains the science and the thought behind the body language we display and how it affects our confidence and power. There are small but significant shifts to improve our confidence that take only minutes and can be done without telling anyone.

> "When you pretend to be powerful, you are more likely to actually be powerful."
>
> ~ Amy Cuddy, Ted Talk: Your Body Language May Shape Who You Are
>
> https://www.ted.com/talks/amy_cuddy_your_body_language_may_shape_who_you_are

4. The Focus On Weaknesses Block

Feelings of not-good-enough, relying on opinions of others to validate our thoughts and actions leads to feelings of disempowerment. You do not need another person to validate what you think or the choices you make. It may feel good and helpful at times to have the validation — however it is not necessary. You want to get to a place of knowing, of feeling secure in your thoughts, beliefs, decisions and actions of what you are doing.

You are so strong in them that you're not affected by another person's agreement or disagreement with you.

Sometimes we make a decision for what we really want and then we don't stick with it because we allow someone to talk us out of it. Or we worry we may be judged for our choice and then someone else's opinion becomes more important than our own. Sound familiar? This is why it is important to have done the work up to this point in the book because by now you have identified what you want in all areas of your life. You know what your values and priorities are. When your thoughts and actions are in alignment with what you've identified that you want for life, you gain the knowing and trust in yourself, your decisions and actions. And you allow those people who are not in alignment with you to fall back and become less impactful on you.

When we focus on what's not working in our lives, what we don't like about ourselves, we can get into a trap of negativity. One that keeps us in the struggle, in a state of low energy. You can learn to shift this easily and quickly once you are aware of it and how to do it.

Dissolving The Focus On Weaknesses Block: This is also known as feelings of not-good-enough and relying on opinions of others. Where the focus is — grows. Identify when you rent room in your mind to spend thinking of your weaknesses. Have you done it today, this week, this month? Or what about the act of ruminating on what other people say you should do with your life? These are the times to catch yourself in the act and shift to thoughts that feel better. And the way you do this is by going back to your list of what you have identified you want for yourself in all areas of your life. Go back to your values and priorities.

Ask, is this action in alignment with the woman you choose to be? You will focus on your weakness less and less and learn to shift to focus on your strengths and where you are going and who you are being and becoming. Also, allow yourself space to be human and make mistakes. And then get back on track as soon as possible. This is not a time to be hard on yourself and judge yourself. You are moving away from that now. It's time to focus on healthy thoughts, healthy actions and moving forward. If you do find a negative thought or action recurring, go back and do one of the exercises specifically for healing hurts. Ask a trusted friend who is knowledgeable in this work or ask a coach to help you move past what is holding you back.

5. Being Inauthentic Block

    When we are not authentic, we also hide our light. And now, more than ever, the world needs your light. We can look at the messaging we've received as girls and as women that has inhibited us from shining our light and being fully empowered in a man's world. Messages such as, it is more important to give than to receive, to sit in the passenger seat instead of driving, to play down your achievements, to not be full of yourself or confident because others won't like you. Those messages breed girls who turn into women who then don't know how to love themselves. They don't know how to receive or accept accomplishments or feel good when achieving goals because there is the underlying fear that putting attention on ourselves is wrong. It's self-serving and that's "bad." "Good girls, nice girls" — they don't do those kinds of things. They focus on others. Do you see how this becomes a vicious cycle and leads to struggle for women?

    Dissolving The Being Inauthentic Block: Ladies, shine your light, no more hiding. Make one move today, big or small to be the authentic YOU. Share one of your accomplishments with another person. Write a list of everything you did in the last week, month or year that you are proud of. The world needs your light. Be the evidence for others of women succeeding, of women winning, of women making an impact in the world. Woman to woman — let's build a world where we cheer on other women. Let's build a world where it's safe to be awesome, successful and happy in all areas of our lives.

The next time you notice the urge to want to tell someone something cool you did or take a photo of yourself and share it, and then you stop or second guess yourself — ask yourself, what am I worried about? And shift to a better thought, one where you are free to shine your light. So often we just never know who needs to see it, who is watching from afar, and whose lives we impact by being a light. Someone out there might need your light in their darkness this very day. Then who becomes more important? The naysayers or the one person who needs to see your light?

Confidence is holding unwavering faith in yourself. Trust in the work you have done up to this point to identify your goals, priorities and values in life. Then trust that by doing that, you will know the right path for you based on your alignment. And then trust that if you get off your path, you can quickly and easily get back on track.

Confidence starts with discomfort. It's like exercise. When you begin a regular practice, you may pull muscles, stretch and feel even silly, or out of your comfort zone. But as you build your practices and stay consistent, your muscles get stronger. It becomes more natural. The growing pains stop one day. It's the same experience with confidence. It becomes less uncomfortable and begins to feel more natural as you practice it.

Chapter 5

Turn Pain into Power

I remember reading the book, *Five Wishes* by Gay Hendricks years ago and experiencing a shift in my thinking. I began to think about my life and the choices I made from the perspective of the end of my life. I got clear on what I wanted and ways I could leave a legacy. It became my guide for making daily decisions and bigger goals I would set. It is an extension of Identify What You Want. While that focus is on the woman you are being daily and becoming long term, this focus is on doing. If you were at the end of your life, what would you want to have done?

What if you can build something bigger than the pain you experienced? What if you can turn your obstacles into opportunities?

That is exactly what Malebogo, from Botswana, Africa did. She was featured in *#SheWins*, because she was shot eight times by her boyfriend. Malebogo was a member of the national basketball team and was paralyzed as a result of the shooting. As you can imagine, she experienced a lot of pain having her passion and livelihood taken from her. But Malebogo healed her hurts and now she leads efforts of inclusion for people with disabilities to play sports. She has held basketball wheelchair tournaments. She was a recipient of the United States Secretary of State's International Women of Courage Award. Malebogo educates the people of Botswana on gender-based violence. She is an excellent example of a woman who's created something bigger than the pain she experienced.

If you knew you could help others from your trauma, experiences and through what you learned about healing and overcoming — could it serve a bigger purpose? Would it make what you went through worth it?

This was the very statement I wrote down in the spring of 2017. Even though it had been five years since I divorced from my abusive marriage, I still felt the after effects of it and the pain of parallel parenting with my children's father. I remember sitting on the couch in my living room, in tears, writing, "If I could just help one woman move beyond domestic abuse — everything I went through would have been worth it." It would have served a larger purpose.

I didn't know what to do at the time, but I felt the strong desire to help at least one other woman by what I went through. Months later, there was a woman at my photography studio saying she helped women write their stories of overcoming abuse. We discussed including photographs with the stories and *#SheWins* was born. All it took was willingness to participate in a conversation and be receptive to the idea. Then courage to take one step in that direction. For me that was asking an acquaintance if he'd be interested in publishing it. And then commitment to follow it through, one piece at a time.

From that one piece, *#SheWins*, I have been able to help hundreds, if not thousands of women. And I can tell you — that alone made everything I went through worth it. It also led to more books and helping more women. My path unfolded and I continued taking one step at a time in the direction of my goals and dreams.

- Dream Big and Keep a Journal.

    How do you begin creating the process of turning your pain into power? By creating a big-picture vision for your life. You'll be happy to know you've already started by Identifying

What You Want. Imagine the woman you're becoming. Who is she five years from now? What is the life she's created in the areas of health, relationships, career, finances, self-development, fun/free time. What impact does she have on others and society? I suggest choosing five of these areas to focus on.

This exercise is meant to help you achieve clarity and help you to live your days in alignment with what you work towards. It is meant to be a guide, a compass for you to use to navigate life. Think about passions, electricity, what excites you? Think about your gifts and your talents. Could you serve on the board of a nonprofit? Or volunteer your time at a shelter or a philanthropic cause that is close to your heart? The world needs your light and you can shine it in multiple ways to be the change we all wish to see. And if you don't know what your gifts and talents are, take time to explore and discover them. Another exercise is to survey 10 people close to you and ask them what your strengths are. Then borrow their beliefs about you until you can believe them on your own as well.

Journaling is my favorite way to work on exercises such as these. I highly encourage you to take time to journal this too. The morning is preferred; I do all of my journaling then. I do it first to make sure that I take that time for myself before other events and appointments fill my day and leave me without the time to spend on my important activities — this is a priority for me.

To take this exercise to another level, you can find a trusted person to discuss what you want to achieve in your life. Also, create a vision board on Pinterest or a physical one with magazines and pictures.

Then take time to really dive into what it is that you want. Imagine your life in 10, 20, 40 years from now. Get excited. Get creative. The key is that you can dream — you don't have to know HOW this is all going to happen. Needing to know the "how" causes us to bring our visions down to something more reasonable. Don't be reasonable now. Reasonability keeps people stuck. Reasonability keeps people playing small. Reasonability doesn't challenge you. Dream and create. Then be open to experiences that surface. They may be the same as you imagined or they may be even better.

It was not reasonable for me to think I could become an author. I wasn't an English major, nor did I have expertise to write a book, or so I thought. I did know I wanted to help women, so I was open to that. And then the domestic abuse book idea came. I realized I did have expertise in overcoming abuse, and it became an opportunity to turn my pain into power. I challenged myself to become a better writer and to be open to building something big. It is now better than I ever thought possible and I am in the process of my fourth book as I write this. I know that these opportunities and more are possible for each of you!

Ask yourself about your big picture vision: What do I do? Who is in my life? What does it look like? What does it feel like? Really step into the shoes of that woman. Feel what it's like to be her in the present tense. Journal about the areas of your life that are important to you as if you are that woman. In doing this — you are creating and calling in your life's experiences. You are choosing instead of waiting to "see what happens to your life." Can you feel the difference? You are being proactive versus reactive. You're choosing empowerment over disempowerment. Whenever you are not making your own choice in your life, someone else is making one for you.

Take your power back. Own it. Feel it. Act as if you have it — until you embody it.

Choose your path. Choose your life experiences.

When you journal on the five areas, include your WHYs. Why do you want what you want? What are the benefits to you? To others? How will you feel? What freedoms will you experience? When we know our why, it helps us to get through the challenges that come along when we take steps in the directions of our dreams. I have never heard someone say, my dreams came true and it was so easy. But when we have the grit and tenacity to navigate our challenges, that's when we can do anything we dream.

Be strong in your "why" so you attain the drive to get to where you're going.

- Reverse the Process.

When you finish journaling, then begin the reverse engineer process. Look at what you want to do, be, have and then create the steps working backwards. Now I know that things may not play out in the same way as the steps you have written — and I want to encourage you to be open to new and different ways your goals can happen. Be open to surprise and delight. But when you begin to think of the process to meet your goal, you let the universe know you are serious and the universe responds.

Learn to distinguish when to say yes and when to say no to opportunities. When I asked my acquaintance if he'd be interested in publishing *#SheWins*, his partner had recently retired from the publishing company and there was an opening available. I took it and I never looked back. I saw it as an opportunity to help more women tell their stories. That was part of my big picture vision, even though I never imagined becoming part of a publishing company. I was open to receive it, it has been an excellent fit for me and now I am CEO of Personal Power Press.

What if you don't know what the steps are? You just know there is something bigger for you. Well, then you are like me, I didn't know the steps. I just knew when the opportunity presented — becoming part of the publishing company — that it was the right fit. It was one step I could make towards something bigger. And at the time, I can say it may not have been a reasonable decision. At the time, I had a photography studio. I was already busy with that and my family. Yet, I just knew. And I trusted my intuition. It came down to trust.

- Make One Move.

What is the next step after the reverse engineer process? Make one move. Make one move in the direction of your goal. If you can make a big move, make a big move. If you can make a small move, then make a small move. I said yes to becoming part of the publishing company. A year after that, I closed my photography studio. And that opened more opportunities to publish more books.

Kayla also made one move from where she was — creating her Facebook Page, *She Rises*. It was one small move which in turn, led to helping others, speaking, writing a book and more.

Another example is if you have included travel on your list as something you want to experience in your life. What is one small move you can make in that direction? Can you open a travel account through your bank and deposit $10 weekly? Can you begin making a list of countries you want to travel to? Can you buy an outfit, a bathing suit or a hat to wear on your trip? Can you look at airfare options? Can you decide who to take with you on a specific trip? Making one move can start with research. Where do you really desire to travel? Get specific on the details. Then make another move from where you are and with the resources you have at the time. And then another move after that. What is incredible about this process is that these small shifts add up and before you know it, they close the gap from where you were to where you want to be. Use this process in all areas of your life where you want to grow.

Have fun with this! The idea is to generate desire in your life. Watch the pieces unfold and reveal themselves to you. As you do this, the gap closes through small shifts, bite-size increments as you walk the path to living your best life. Trust the process will unfold in the best way for you and trust in yourself to make the right decisions as it does.

Chapter 6

Relationship Red Flags vs Mistakes

When Kayla and I were talking towards the end of writing this book, she asked me, "How do you know if a boyfriend is just making a mistake or if it's a red flag?" She wanted to feel trust with future relationships rather than constant questioning if his every move meant he would become abusive.

Red flags signal something is toxic in a relationship. Could a mistake be perceived as a red flag also? I want to list some behaviors of healthy relationships. These behaviors are not found in toxic or abusive relationships and this is how you can determine the difference. Everyone is human and capable of making mistakes. However — in a healthy relationship, the following behaviors are consistent:

- Your partner sees the best in you. He doesn't point out your mistakes to shame and blame you.

- He/she encourages your life/interests/time outside of the relationship as well as in the relationship. He doesn't demand all your time and attention or isolate you from your friends and family.

- He/she encourages you to be your own person. He doesn't monopolize your time, belittle your capabilities, or make "the couple" more important than the individual.

- He is a "whole" person with his own interests and invests in his development as an individual. Healthy relationships are based on two people who grow as individuals and together.

- He/she makes time for people and things that are important to you. It's not just about his/her interests, family and friends only.

- He/she respects your boundaries and your time. If you say "no," you are respected for your decision and he does not manipulate, control, or force you otherwise.

- He/she takes responsibility for their actions. They say I'm sorry when appropriate and make amends for their mistakes. They do not place blame and fault on others.

- Their words and their actions match. If they say they are going to do something, they do it. If they say they are sorry, their actions change to reflect it. They are trustworthy. If they make a promise, they keep it.

- You feel a general sense of well-being when with this person. You like who you are — the way you act, the way you think, the way you talk when you are with this person. When you spend time with this person, you feel in alignment with the person you want to be.

- Your opinions and thoughts are valued. He doesn't try to change them, make you think like him, or wear you down. You don't feel confused and pulled in different directions. There is an equal balance of power, energy and intelligence.

*If you are concerned for your safety and need immediate assistance, call or visit the National Domestic Violence Hotline, https://www.thehotline.org/ or 800.799.SAFE (7233).

Chapter 7

Final Words

We believe you can do hard things.

Use Kayla and me as evidence. Use women you know personally or throughout history as evidence that you too can turn your pain into power and your obstacles into opportunities. It has happened for others and it can happen for you.

There is no one more worthy of receiving good things than you are.

Use this phrase, repeat it to yourself, write it on sticky notes and put them where you can see this message throughout your day and remember:

"I am worthy of the very best things in life, and I am open to receiving them now."

Heal your hurts and use the steps in this book to overcome. Read it once, twice, or three times until these practices become your beliefs. Journal for clarity — there is so much power available to you through this regular practice. The world needs to see your light now more than ever — it is your time to shine.

Kayla and I would love to continue the conversation of healing and overcoming with you.

Please join us in our private Facebook group, *She Rises Book with Kayla & Alisa* :

https://www.facebook.com/groups/387687765935431

Cheers to — your rising — and wearing your scars as wings!

Kayla Hayes & Alisa Divine

About The Authors

Kayla Hayes is 22 years old and an advocate, speaker and author. She rose like an angel and walked away from a past filled with childhood sexual abuse and teenage domestic violence. The tragedies she endured stole her identity, her self-worth, and her confidence. She had two choices: succumb to them or rise from them. Kayla chose to rise — and wear her scars as wings.

Kayla has been featured on *Inside Edition, Cosmopolitan Magazine, #SheWins,* and in multiple national podcasts, interviews and speaking engagements to tell her story and raise domestic violence awareness.

Now she inspires other young people to rise, heal their hurts and wear their scars as wings too.

Visit https://www.sheriseswithkaylahayes.com to book a speaking engagement, a Zoom book tour, or work with her.

Alisa Divine coaches women to tell their stories, build platforms as leaders and create impact through books and businesses. She is CEO of Personal Power Press, the author of *#SheWins* and co-author of *Killing Kate* and *She Rises*.

In addition, Alisa founded *The More Than Beautiful Project™*. Through this program she mentors women and teens to build confidence, develop a positive mindset and choose healthy relationships. She has been a guest expert featured in global summits, conferences, TV, print media, SiriusXM, iHeart Media, Entercom, Florida Public Radio and in several big cities from Boston and Detroit to Minneapolis and San Diego.

Alisa is on the Board of Directors of the Saginaw Underground Railroad, which serves survivors of domestic violence. She lives in Michigan with her husband and their blended family. Visit www.alisadivine.com to book a speaking engagement, a Zoom book tour, or to seek her help in publishing your own story.